TWENTY THOUSAND SHOTS

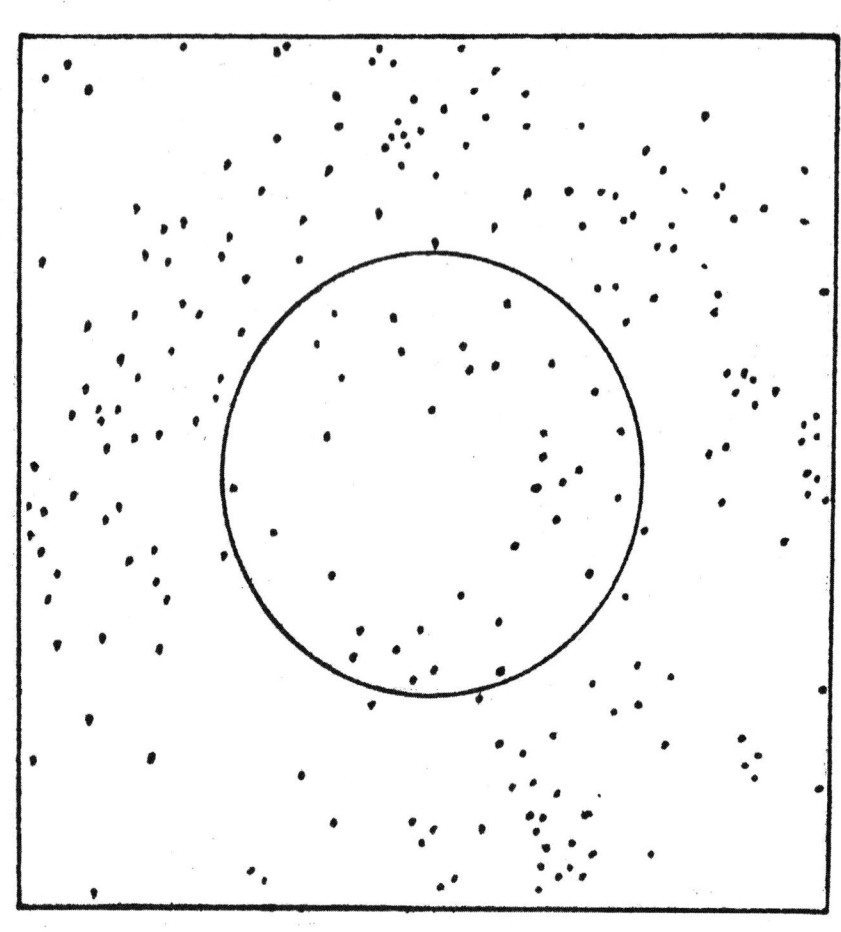

A TYPICAL "CARTWHEEL" PATTERN AT 40 YARDS

TWENTY THOUSAND SHOTS

*The writings of a remarkable
Victorian amateur ballistician*

Compiled with Commentary
by
DAVID J BAKER

With Original Illustrations
by
Mary Ann Gelly

COCH-Y-BONDDU BOOKS
2018

For Lynne, with thanks

TWENTY THOUSAND SHOTS
By DAVID J BAKER

Copyright © Coch-y-Bonddu Books, 2018
Text © David J Baker, 2018
Illustrations © Mary Ann Gelly, 2018

ISBN 978 1 904784 86 9

Coch-y-Bonddu Books Ltd,
Machynlleth, Powys SY20 8DG
01654 702837
www.anglebooks.com

*All rights reserved.
No part of this publication may be reproduced,
stored in a retrieval system, or transmitted, in any form
or by any means, electronic, mechanical, photocopying,
recording or otherwise, without the prior consent
of the copyright holder.*

Printed by TJ International Ltd, Padstow, Cornwall

Contents

Who was 20,000 Shots?	9
A.J. Lane and *The Sporting Mirror*	11
Arthur James Lane – a portrait from *The Field*	13
A.J. Lane's Claim to Fame	19
Notes on the 'Sporting Reminiscences and Anecdotes'	20

Part One
SPORTING REMINISCENCES AND ANECDOTES

Sporting Reminiscences and Anecdotes I–XVI	25

Part Two
THE LETTERS

Letter of Reminiscence	137
The First Letter to *The Field*	140
The Inventions of A.J. Lane	143
A.J. Lanes's Investigation of the Ball and Shotgun	149
The Field Trials and the Choke Bore	155
Weston's of Brighton	161
A.J. Lane – Shotgun Ballistician	163
Modern Gunpowders	165
A.J. Lane on Cartridge Loading	176
Schultze	179
Experimental and Special Cartridges	182
Jones' Wad Press	185

How to Load a Gun	187
The Kynoch 'Perfect' Cartridge Case	198
Ford's Cartridges	209
'The Guns of our Ancestors' Trial	212
Guns, Gun Barrels and Gunmaking	217
How to Choose a Gun	223
The Hammerless Gun and the Silver's Safety	234
The Last Letter to *The Field*	239

Part Three
APPENDICES

I	Milestones in the Life of A.J. Lane	245
II	Obituaries	247
III	A.J. Lane's Letters to *The Field*	249
IV	Notes from A.J. Lane's Letters to *The Field*	255
V	Other Writings by A.J. Lane	259

Preface

The following has been a retirement project, written in very large measure, for my own enjoyment. The motivation came from the simple fact that, on many levels, I empathise with Arthur Lane. His enthusiasm, inventiveness and practical approach I find particularly appealing.

Likewise, his kindliness is a quality that comes over in many ways, from training Sancho with the just reward of what sounds like a delightful companion, to the long trip to test a gun in his old age. A man whose company I would very much enjoy.

Inevitably, the selection of Arthur's writings presented here reflects my own theories and interests. That said, I believe there is much we can all learn from his experience.

Given the lapse of time since the events took place, inevitably much has been lost. What we do have are tantalising references, the guns he made, his paintings and, above all, his Shooting Journals. It is probably unrealistic to hope that any of the missing material might surface, but who knows? More hope may be entertained as to the reason why, late in life, he adopted the second surname of 'Norton'. What may be a clue here is that this was the name of friends of Jane Lane in Bristol who sheltered her and King Charles. Did some link persist down the years?

If publication of this survey turns up significant finds, I promise to do my best to write a supplement to this account.

For the present, I hope that you enjoy reading this collection as much as I have enjoyed assembling it.

David Baker 2018

Acknowledgements

I would like to thank the following for their assistance in the production of this book: Mark Crudgington, Sarah Godfrey, Robin Knowles, Paul Morgan, Paul Mosse and Tony Pincott. Special thanks also to Mary Ann Gelly for her illustrations which were specially commissioned for the book.

The following institutions were also consulted during my research: The British Library, the National Library of Wales and the Natural History Museum.

Who Was '20,000 Shots'?

The short answer is Arthur James Lane, 1816–1906. 'One who has Fired 20,000 Shots at Marks' was the pseudonym adopted to reflect his lifelong evaluation of the exterior ballistics of sporting shotguns. With the exception of the story of the family's involvement with the escape of King Charles, the sporting reminiscences and family history were probably little different from many others of his social standing.

What sets these apart is that they were written down. He had the good fortune to spend idyllic teenage years in the 1830s, living some 20 miles east of what is now Gatwick airport, when the area was sparsely populated and served only by dirt roads. Not only were there no railways, there was no civil registration of births, marriages and deaths, and no photography. In other words, we are faced with a dearth of surviving information.

The style of shooting that he enjoyed led him to advocate in later life a type of gun that was both short barrelled and heavily choked – a combination which would not sell well today.

The survival of his memoirs is due to the phenomenon that was *The Field*. That a weekly newspaper became almost a national institution is a complex and fascinating story in its own right. Suffice it to say that, within a decade of its first appearance in 1853, *The Field* had become a highly respected forum for all sorts of topics related to the countryside, shooting being but one of these. It was a reflection of the lifestyle of the contributors that a goodly proportion of the content of the shooting section consisted of long letters written by readers, for which they were not paid. Of these contributors, a relatively small number became regulars and, from the soundness of their views, became regarded as experts in their topics.

The niche colonised by Arthur Lane was that of studying the external ballistics of a shotgun, and he had a ready-made audience because the greater proportion of his readers had shot with a muzzle loading shotgun. As a result, they had gained firsthand experience of the choice of components and the effects these had on the performance of their guns.

With a letter-writing career spanning nearly forty years, 173 letters and some 120,000 words, Arthur Lane became something of an institution and, as a result, was persuaded to write his memoirs at the very end of his writing career.

It is to be regretted that he stopped when he did, considering that he had experienced firsthand the evolution of the sporting gun from flintlock to hammerless ejector. What a tale he could have told! We have fragments in his letters, which only serve to tantalize. For instance, as will be seen, with his championship of the "Silver" safety, we have a glimpse of his earlier experiences with various safety systems.

Lane was a descendant of the Lanes of Bentley Hall near Walsall, an ancient and wealthy family, well-known for having sheltered Charles II overnight after his defeat at the battle of Worcester in 1651. The King was helped by Colonel John Lane and his sister Jane Lane; Jane took him, disguised as her servant, to Bristol from where he continued his escape to France. A.J. Lane, together with his older brother, Farindon, was heir to property and mineral rights at Moseley Hole Estate, close to the site of the former Bentley Hall.

A.J. Lane and *The Sporting Mirror*[*]

Finding the following biographical entry in *The Sporting Mirror* of December 1882 was an important boost for the project. That it was written in Arthur Lane's lifetime, and presumably with his co-operation and approval, are important, but the greatest value lies in the portrait, which was a feature of all *The Sporting Mirror* biographies.

The articles that Lane wrote for this publication are significant because, while they often cover points raised in his letters to *The Field*, *The Sporting Mirror* pieces are more rounded in their treatment of their subject.

In view of his long-standing association with *The Field*, it is possible that he was viewed as a 'catch' by the editorial staff of the new magazine, which first appeared in 1881.

No matter what the nuances of the contemporary politics, since the biography contains important material not readily available from any other source, we have no hesitation in re-publishing it in full.

---

[*] *The Sporting Mirror* was a monthly magazine published between 1881 and 1885. Its main focus was on the personalities of 'The Turf', but with a fair coverage of athletics. In its earlier years, there was a limited shooting content, which sadly diminished over the lifetime of the publication.

ONE WHO HAS FIRED SOME 20,000 TRIAL SHOTS AT MARKS.

ARTHUR JAMES LANE

IT IS VERY probable that our readers will not recognise the subject of our portrait by the name under which he is known in private life and amongst his friends. However, in the world of guns and gunning few are better known; one has only to mention the name of "One who has Fired Some 20,000 Trial Shots at Marks" to command universal attention. This curious synonym is the name by which Mr. Lane has worked and written, and all will thus recognise him not only as a contributor to the columns of the SPORTING MIRROR, but as the author of the many interesting and practical articles which have appeared in the pages of our contemporaries. In the gunning world alone his position stands second to none in the knowledge of a gun and how to use it, whilst the mechanism and everything appertaining to the manufacture thereof has been a lifelong study.

Mr. Arthur James Lane, better known as "One who has Fired Some 20,000 Trial Shots at Marks," was born in March, 1816. He comes of a good old English and somewhat sporting family, viz., the Lanes, of Bentley, of King Charles II notoriety, but, being descended from one of the younger branches, does not quarter the white horse in his arms. His family was well-known in the old days, and many of his ancestors have served their king and country with honour and distinction. During a long life Mr. Lane has been connected with the gun, and has had the advantage of seeing this weapon pass through many stages of development, from the crude form of the old flint-lock to the now highly-finished hammerless. Its study has been the great hobby of his life, and it would be difficult to find another private gentleman who has the whole science, theory, and practice of the shot-gun more thoroughly at command.

From his earliest boyhood he was the constant companion of the gamekeeper, going his rounds regularly, and by the time he entered his teens was not only a good shot, but a fairly experienced trapper. Here he picked up that intimate knowledge of the habits of game and vermin which have been so useful to him in after life. Thus few men could lay out and beat a country with a view to making the most of the game upon it with greater skill and judgment. At the early age of fourteen he commenced game-shooting regularly, and has been ever a constant votary of the gun. It was the custom at his father's house, before the commencement of each shooting season, to put every gun in the establishment through a regular series of target trials, to see if any had deteriorated during the past year's wear. These trials were now left pretty much in the hands of the subject of this sketch, and he soon began taking notes of anything remarkable that occurred during their working. This soon gave way to the system of noting the full particulars of each individual shot, and laid the foundation of a vast accumulation of trial shots, which has given rise to the signature by which he has latterly been so well known.

Soon after the establishment of the *Field* he commenced as a free correspondent to address letters on guns and shooting to that celebrated journal, at first under the signature of "One who has Fired Some 10,000 Trial Shots at Marks"; but after a time, finding this did not represent the facts, he increased the number to "20,000," which he has continued ever since, though probably double that number would scarcely now represent the trial shots actually fired from his own shoulder. For a great number of years it has been the practice among his numerous friends on buying a new gun to send it at once to "20,000 Shots," by which *sobriquet* he has been long known among his intimates, with a request that he would try it and report on its powers, and even a great many strangers have done the same thing. This practice has thrown the guns of almost every maker of repute of the last half-century into his hands, and given him a knowledge of what may be expected from the different factories, which few other men had a similar chance of acquiring. He has always been most courteous and ready to reply to all inquiries and to give every information in his power alike to the experienced sportsman or the veriest tyro. In addition, he has always made public everything that he thought would prove useful to his brother sportsmen. About the year 1840, Mr. Lane was the first to hit upon the plan of lining nipples with platinum. This he at once made public, and in a short time it was generally adopted by the leading makers, and remained in general use until the breechloader superseded the cap gun, and he has now in his possession the first pair of nipples ever so lined. He was also the inventor of the paper concentrators, subsequently brought out by Mr. Charles Lancaster, he having used them and freely distributed them for several years previously. Mr. Lane also invented a military breechloading rifle at the time of the Crimean War. Besides these, several other suggestions have emanated from him and have been partially or wholly adopted by the gun trade at various times, and his opinion has been sought on the many new inventions connected with the gun. Mr. Lane has been present at all the *Field* gun trials, except the first, usually in the capacity of one of their committee of sportsmen, and we believe his great experience on these occasions was of some little value and assistance.

There can be little doubt that his letters in the *Field* have attracted a considerable amount of attention among sportsmen, as for some years he has had a large correspondence with gentlemen seeking advice or information at his hands, not only in England, but from almost all parts of the world where the English language is spoken.

About four years ago Mr. Lane had the great misfortune to lose the use of his right eye, from suffusion of blood on the retina, and had to take to the use of cross-eyed guns, but could never recover his old form. That he could previously hold his own with field shots of his day, there is little doubt. In proof of this, we can state that on the last two days' shooting he had before the loss of his eye, out of fifty-four shots he killed fifty-one and bagged fifty; and this, too, at the end of the season. It is now much feared that he will never be again able to enjoy any of his favourite sports, as, unfortunately, he is now rapidly losing the sight of the other eye. In his younger days, Mr. Lane was very successful as a dog-breaker, employing a system very closely allied to that subsequently advocated by General Hutchinson in his excellent work on this subject; but he taught his puppies nearly all their work, save quartering their ground, in a walled garden in which were kept a partridge, a pheasant, a hare, and a rabbit. The plan is an admirable one in every way, and the hint may be worth the notice of anyone wishing to break his own dogs.

In addition to his love for guns Mr. Lane has been an enthusiastic yachtsman, but circumstances have always kept him out of large boats, but he was for several years rear or vice-commodore of the Thames Sailing Club, during which time he kept a racer and took the most lively interest in the numerous races of this little sporting club. He never missed a match if he could possibly get to it, and carefully reported them in the columns of the *Field*. As a fisherman he was at one time pretty well known as a Thames spinner, fishing generally with Johnson, or the once famous Bill Wisdom, but for the last seven or eight-and-twenty years he has confined himself to the fly, fishing generally with one old, tried, and highly esteemed friend, who is one of the best fly-fishers in England, and together they have captured several thousand brace of trout. Mr. Lane always tyed (sic) his own flies for both trout and salmon, until his unfortunate loss of sight precluded this. It must not be supposed that all Mr. Lane's ability lies in what may be termed the field of sport. He is a really good mechanic and workman, possessing all the necessary tools for gun manufacturing. So proficient is he in the use thereof, that he has manufactured weapons entirely without aid, and has shot for many ears with guns of his own make. It is somewhat remarkable that Mr. Lane, with all his strong sporting proclivities, and although his grandfather was pretty largely on the turf, keeping racers as well as foxhounds, should never have shewn the slightest inclination for any of the sports pertaining to the saddle. But for this he might have been considered a complete "all-round" man, as in addition to his being a thorough sportsman in other respects, he has been a good amateur painter, musician, and mechanic. This is evidenced by his having at different times exhibited in various galleries in London and elsewhere, and by his having sung as a tenor soloist at numerous amateur concerts given for charities and local institutions, &c.

It is, perhaps, a little remarkable that with the vast amount of trial shooting as well as sport in the field that this gentleman has gone through with guns of every description from the commonest to the best that money could buy, he has never through life met with the slightest accident. This speaks well of his judgment in the use of such varied weapons, and we can only express our regret that this dear lover of sport should so unhappily be compelled to lay aside his gun, being, in all other respects, as "fit" as he was twenty years ago.

Sporting Mirror, December, 1882

A.J. LANE'S FAMILY CREST

In the absence of an accurate family tree, it is not certain whether Arthur Lane had the right to use this crest, together with the associated coat of arms and the motto: *Gardez le Roy*.

That said, based on the claim in *The Sporting Mirror* biography, it would seem that he was part of the greater family to which Jane Lane, who had earned this crest and associated motto by her crucial role in the escape of King Charles II after the battle of Worcester, belonged.

This illustration was scanned from a book plate.

A.J. Lane's Claim to Fame

Arthur Lane's 'Sporting Reminiscences' were written at the very end of his writing career, so it could be argued that they should be at the end of this study. They have been put first, however, because it is my intention to tell Arthur's story chronologically. The order in which the components of this piece were published is but another example of the phenomenon that "young men do things and old men write about what they did when they were young".

At first glance, it appears that there is a gap of thirty or so years between the end of the Reminiscences and the start of *The Field* letters. This is not really so because, in *The Sporting Mirror*, we learn of his sailing, singing and painting. The letters, published in *The Field* record the gunmaking, pattern testing and some shooting experiences. These follow in the second section of this book.

We, selfishly, may lament the lack of much detail in stories of his other pursuits and regret the absence of a diary. Reading between the lines, it is my belief that Arthur was far too busy for such an enterprise and we should be grateful for the archive that he did leave, some of which is recorded in the following pages.

Given the volume of his letter writing on shooting, it is remarkable that, to date, no published material on any other of his hobbies or pastimes has come to light. Perhaps he had other pseudonyms? If so, it would take a huge stroke of luck to gain access to such material. Who knows what might thereby be found?

Notes on the 'Sporting Reminiscences and Anecdotes'

Finding these in *The Field* when engaged in the trawl that was part of my research for *The British Shotgun* was the starting point for this study.

The sixteen 'Sporting Reminiscences and Anecdotes' are the reason that this book came into being. That the Lane family had left the property where the story took place half a century before these pieces were written, makes the deliberate obscurity surrounding its location all the more puzzling.

So started the first of many research projects set in motion by this investigation. The upshot was finding the house called Farindons in Dormansland, Surrey, close to Lingfield Park racecourse.

I think it remarkable that this collection of essays is not more widely known, or indeed has not been previously published, taking the reader, as they do, back to an England that has now largely vanished under suburban sprawl with traffic and aircraft noise.

It seems scarcely credible that the events described happened less than 200 years ago.

A point that perhaps needs to be made here is that this series of articles was written close to the end of Lane's writing career when he was eighty two years old.

PART ONE

12-BORE 2¼-INCH TRUE CYLINDER AT 30 YARDS
Load: 33 grains Smokeless Diamond and 1 1/16 ounce of No. 6

Sporting Reminiscences and Anecdotes

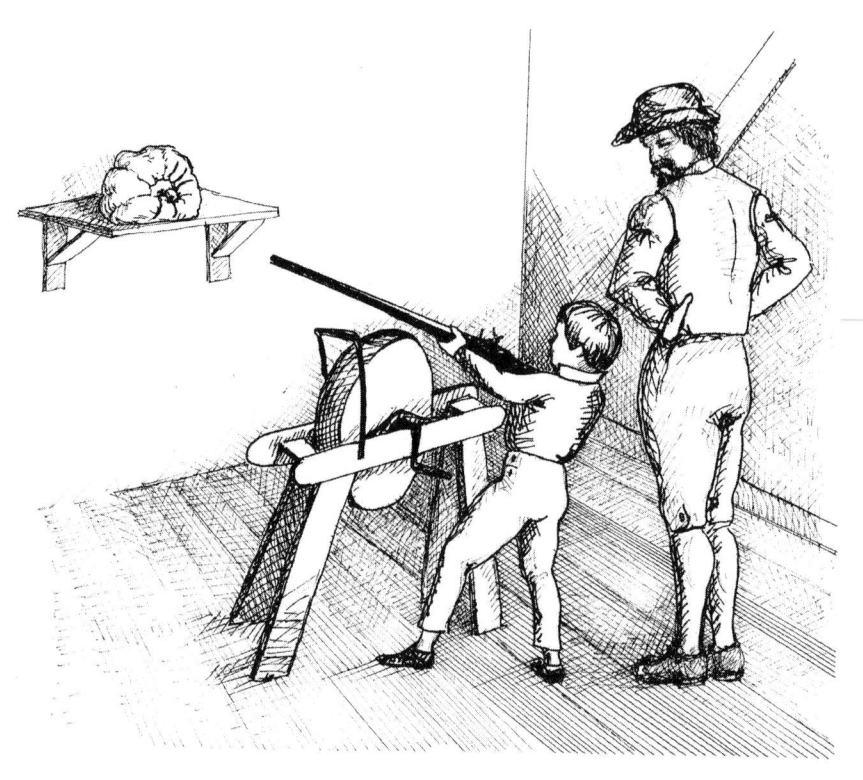

THE FIRST SHOT

SPORTING REMINISCENCES AND ANECDOTES I
BY "20,000 SHOTS"

IN THE COURSE of the last ten or a dozen years I have several times been asked why I did not jot down for publication some of the incidents and experiences of my long sporting career. But I could never induce myself to entertain the idea, from the fear that I might not possess sufficient literary power and ability to carry out such an undertaking. Recently, however, the matter has again been brought before me, and this time by a gentleman of well-known literary talent; and, encouraged by his representations and assurances, I have undertaken to enter upon the work.

Nevertheless, I fear that I may not be able to offer to the reader much that is new, for I feel proud to be able to say that, for the last forty-five years or so, whenever I have, by experiment or otherwise, been fortunate enough to find out anything which would be likely to be useful or interesting to my brother sportsmen, I have always at once made it public – for the most part through the columns of the *Field*, of which journal, I believe, I am at present the oldest of its free correspondents. However, I venture to hope that I may be the means of enabling some readers to pleasantly pass away a leisure half-hour or so, at times when they cannot be following their own favourite recreation by flood and field.

On considering the best manner in which to set out my reminiscences, I think the most convenient way will be to put them in the form of a gossiping, chatty, and anecdotal kind of autobiography. In order to do so I shall begin at the beginning, and say that I descended from families of thorough sportsmen upon both sides. My paternal grandfather was a man of considerable fortune, coming of a well-known Staffordshire family, which was very instrumental in securing the escape of King Charles after the disastrous battle of Worcester, through the courage and tact of a lady who passed off his Majesty as Will Jackson, her groom. But this story is told much better than I can possibly hope to do by Harrison Ainsworth, in his romance of "Boscobel."

My grandfather, after inheriting another considerable fortune, through the death of a brother, married one of the richest heiresses at that time in England, and was possessed of a fine income, which amounted to over £26,000 a year. Alas, however, he was too much of a sportsman; he kept and hunted the Surrey Foxhounds at his own expense, went on the Turf, and dropped over £30,000 over his first Derby, and continuing the same dangerous course soon made "ducks and drakes" of his large fortune, and at his death nothing was left but a small freehold in Middlesex.

A curious incident occurred one day, while he was drawing a small plantation for a fox, on the right of Smitham Bottom, on the road leading to Riddlesdown. My grandmother was driving along the road when a gentleman, attended by his groom, rode up to the carriage, raised his hat, and remained for some minutes talking to her (the groom remaining at the horses' heads). He then again raised his hat, and rode off in the direction of Riddlesdown. All this occurred within a quarter of a mile of my grandfather and his friends, he remarking to one of them, "Who the deuce has my wife got hold of there? I don't know but he seems a gentleman at any rate." On his return home to dinner he was soon informed that this *gentleman,* with his groom in livery, were two highwaymen, who, who had relieved my grandmother of her watch and chain, several diamond and other rings, brooches and bracelets, and her purse. But before leaving her he had returned one shilling, "as he had not the honour of knowing where she lived, and she might have to go through the turnpike at Croydon, and he could not think of inconveniencing her, by causing here to be detained at the gate!"

I cannot resist telling another anecdote of my grandfather. He was visiting some property near Mosely, in Staffordshire, when he one day came across a burly miner, over six feet in height, with arms like a blacksmith, belabouring his wretched wife in a most brutal manner. On my grandfather interfering, the miner threatened to pitch him over the hedge. "Oh!" said my grandfather, "you may hurt yourself at that game," and on the miner attempting to carry out his threat, found he had woefully misjudged his man, who, though rather a short man, was as active as a squirrel, and, moreover, had the reputation of being one of the most powerful, as well as one of the most scientific, of amateur bruisers in the metropolis. The result was that in a few minutes the giant miner was so thrashed that probably his own wife would not have known him had she met him casually. Seeing this, the wife, on whose behalf my grandfather had interfered, deliberately took her pattens from her feet, seized him by the queue (then universally worn by gentlemen) with her left hand, exclaimed "D——n your eyes! Is that the way you treat my husband," and began banging his head with the iron rings of the pattens, while her husband was doing his best to punish him in front; but his eyes were so effectually "banged up," he could do but little and my grandfather soon succeeded in shaking both off, when the miner received a blow in the face that deposited him helpless in the ditch; and my grandfather retired, vowing never again to "interfere between husband and wife."

But he was none the worse, saving a few bruises on the head from the pattens. Verily, you may stuff people with everything but gratitude.

My father, who was the eldest of seven children, was born in 1773 at Selsdon, one of the fine estates of my grandmother and which was, until quite lately, for many years the residence of the late Archbishop of Canterbury. Here my father spent his boyhood, and I have heard him say that, when at school in Croydon, he was taken out of a night to see the light of the fires in London caused by the Lord George Gordon rioters.

When he was about seventeen he showed so much tact and skill in collecting and getting up evidence, in a heavy lawsuit in which my grandfather was engaged, and the solicitors were so pleased with him that they offered him a seat in their office as an articled clerk. Well knowing his father's terrible gambling propensities, he at once jumped at the offer, fearing that, as matters were going, there would be little or nothing left for him as the eldest son. So he became a solicitor, and in a few years after entering the profession he was well known, and had a very large practice in London. But although he was a lawyer, he was always a thorough sportsman, and was certainly one of the best shots and one of the best fly fishermen I ever saw.

My mother was a member of a very old Surrey family – also a race of thorough sportsmen – and I made my appearance in this very pleasant world on March 14, in the year 1816, and was the youngest of four children; alas! I am now the only one left.

My earliest recollections are associated with dogs, guns, and fishing-rods – in fact, I have really lived all my life in an atmosphere of sport. The first toy that I have any vivid recollection of was a toy gun of French manufacture, bought for me by my mother at the Soho Bazaar, when I was about six years old. How well I recollect that gun! It had an iron barrel and a very fair flintlock; the stock had a carved duck's head at the handle, the crown of the head forming something like a pistol grip to the handle of the gun; while the bill lay along, under the butt of the gun. How proud I was of this toy! And what was my delight when my father would sometimes put a little pinch of powder into the pan for me to fire! How well I remember all the delight it gave me to see the tiny flash, and watch the smoke go curling up. And then he would show me how to wipe out the pan to prevent its rusting, and instruct me how to handle it, so that the muzzle should never be pointed towards anyone.

Soon after this my father acquired some property in Surrey, and on this built a very comfortable and pretty house, surrounded by lovely, undulating gardens and shrubberies; and here the happiest days of my boyhood were spend. He also rented a large tract of covert and shooting, and secured the services of my grandfather's old gamekeeper, who taught me to shoot – and right well he did the work. A better gamekeeper or more honest man never looked after a major. Dead old Sam Wood! While I write this, feelings of the greatest pleasure and gratification fill my mind; he was so thoroughly reliable, truthful and trustworthy.

My father, of course, shot regularly, and in those days of flint guns it was always the custom to squib off some powder in the guns before loading; and long before I could hold a gun to be certain of not dropping it, it was held by one hand by my father, while I put it to my shoulder and squibbed it off, the same process devolving on me on his return in the evening, after the shot had been drawn out.

When I was about eight years old Sam Wood asked me whether I had "ever fired a gun with shot in it?" To which I replied, breathlessly, "No!" He then said, "Come along with me any you shall have a shot now." He took me down to the potting shed behind the melon frames, and put a very light load into the gardener's gun, a rough, old article, with a very light, thin barrel, except at the breech end, where there was plenty of metal, and it was fitted with an old musket lock.

The next thing was "What was I to shoot at?" And the gardener suggested a seed pumpkin which was lying on a shelf at the other end of the shed. Sam then proceeded to lay the gun on the stage of a large grindstone, to act as a rest, and, having carefully levelled the gun at the pumpkin, said: "Now, Master Arthur, come and take the gun, put your shoulder to the butt without moving it, look steadily along the barrel with both eyes open, and pull the trigger." I replied, "Sam, I would much rather hold the gun for myself," and, taking it from the rest I threw it up to my shoulder and fired. To his great delight, and my own, too, I smashed a hole as big as his fist in the pumpkin, which was end on to me. He immediately said: "Take that in and show your ma." But I thought "better not," as I feared an interdict would be put on my shooting anything more than powder. However, the matter soon leaked out, and from that time I was allowed an occasional shot under the keeper's care and discretion; and, by the time I was twelve years old, I was a very fair shot on the wing, being able to knock over blackbirds and thrushes with commendable certainty, as they flew from the currant and gooseberry bushes in the fruit garden.

The Field, April 2nd 1898

SPORTING REMINISCENCES AND ANECDOTES II
BY "20,000 SHOTS"

HOW WELL DO I REMEMBER my first shot at a partridge! I was not above ten or eleven when, to my great delight, my dear old father said, "Now, instead of squibbing the gun, I'd put a little shot in, and you shall walk with me and have a shot at a lark," and, to my astonishment, I was allowed to carry the loaded gun myself all the way. We went into a heath field near the house, and walked down for thirty or forty yards or so before finding a lark, when up rose a small covey of birds from almost under my feet. My father immediately called out, "Shoot, Arthur, shoot!" The gun was instantly thrown to my shoulder and fired, and down came the outside bird, my father exclaiming, "By Jove, you did that well; and the outside bird, too." Turning to the keeper, he said, "Sam, you are teaching that boy well; and if he goes on like this he'll make a ripping shot."

While he was reloading, the keeper retrieved, and brought in the bird. My dear old dad put it into my hand, saying, "Take that home to your mother and show her what you have done; I'll go after the rest and get some of them." I believe I could have cuddled that bird as I walked home, a proud and happy boy, to show my mother my first partridge. I need hardly say how pleased she was too.

In these days of breechloaders, hammerless ejectors, &c., I suspect a vast number of my readers will have no idea what a business loading was between sixty and seventy years ago.

At this time Forsythe's detonator was but just out (so that nearly all men used flint and steel). This invention was a magazine lock, the magazine being hinged to the hammer, and in falling deposited a small amount of detonating powder over the opening communicating with the barrel; this, on being struck by the hammer, was fired, and flashed into the charge. But these locks were found to be dangerous, for when worn, the magazine occasionally blew up.

Then came the patch locks; my brother shot with one for several years. These, in wet weather, were as liable to miss fire as the old flint and steel. After this tube guns, and the splendid copper cap guns; with this some people thought the acme of sporting guns was arrived at, and they certainly were admirable.

About the year 1845, I hit upon the idea of lining the bottom of the nipples with platinum, leaving a very small flash hole. The result of this was a much quicker and surer ignition. If a spot of wet fell on the metal it did not soak into the powder and cause a miss or hang fire. As usual I made this public, and, in about a year, they were made by most of the best gunmakers. I still have by me the first pair of nipples ever made in this way, and, though used for years, they are as good now as when they were first put into the gun.

Between sixty and seventy years ago, loads were mostly one part by measure of powder and two parts of shot, twice as much shot as powder. (What would be said of this now?) The shooter having dropped in the powder, rammed down a good lump of softish brown paper, doing the same after the shot. I well recollect that many farmers at this time carried the bowl of an ordinary tobacco pipe (not a big "churchwarden"), which was filled with powder once and twice with shot; this, with the lumps of brown paper, caused the ramrod to stand a good five fingers above the muzzle, and was measured by placing the hand, with the fingers altogether (near the knuckles) against the ramrod, and if it stood some half inch or so above the first finger the load was all right.

After this the use of wadding came in, cut with a punch to fit the bore, from an old beaver hat; but the brown paper was still used over the shot, and this reduced the load to only four fingers; a pretty good lump it was, too, to put into a 15 or 16 bore, then mostly used; though many guns were as small as 22 gauge, but, so far as I recollect, the load was about the same, and but few men carried a double-barrel.

At this time my father always used steel chargers, the smaller end being used for the powder, and it was my business, as a youngster walking with him, to keep these filled.

Soon after this a sheet wadding was introduced; a soft, pastboardy substance, nearly an eighth of an inch thick; this was thought a very great improvement, and much resembled what was afterwards sold ready cut in boxes, and known as "Baldwin's Wadding." It was part of my duty, during the summer, to punch out some thousands of these wads for the different guns.

At this period it was commonly the custom to put a small square of stiff brown paper only over the shot; and it had one advantage, certainly, as a man *must* carry his muzzle up, or run the risk of the shot loosening and rolling out at the muzzle. Of course, this was useless in a double gun, so card wadding on the shot was introduced, and soon became general, and many a pack of old playing cards have I cut up for this purpose. At first there was some fun attached to their use, inasmuch as, in forcing them down, the compressed air in the barrel would drive the wadding many inches back up towards the muzzle; and if the thumb and finger slipped off the rod, away it would fly a yard or so into the air. Then someone hit on the idea of boring a small hole near the centre of each card wad, and this ended that difficulty.

Loading, in the days of flint locks, was a work of time as well as art. After a shot, the first process was to brush out the pan with a pocket brush, carried for the purpose. To the centre of this brush was tied a strip of linen, nearly an inch wide, and about eight or ten long; the pan, hammer, and flint were then wiped with this, and the finger nail drawn across the flint also. Sometimes, if the flint was an old one, the striking edge of it was rubbed with a piece of stone brimstone. A pin was then inserted into the touchhole, the pan filled up with the brush rag, and the hammer closed upon it, the gun being at half cock.

Then commenced the process of loading and then the hammer was thrown back, the rag removed, and the pin withdrawn. A look was given to see that all was clean, and the pan carefully filled with powder (but not to repletion) from a small priming flask carried for the purpose. The pan was then carefully closed, the gun turned lock upwards and given two or three thumps with the palm of the right hand, to shake some of the powder through the touchhole, so as to communicate with the charge inside, and then the party was ready to move on.

Think of this, ye shooters of the present day, who go out with three guns and men to put the cartridges in for you. Nevertheless, the sport in those days was as much more enjoyable and health-giving, and in advance of the present style, as foxhunting is before rathunting. Then, every man who carried a gun knew the habits of every kind of game as perfectly as he knew his own fields, and in what way to set about circumventing their wiles and cunning tricks, and I shrewdly suspect a good many shooters of the present day are not satisfied unless they are constantly firing their guns, until they get too hot to hold; and it must be confessed we old-fashioned shooters cannot see the sport of this "slaughter of the innocent."

But the days of heavy loading were not passed at the times I was before alluding to. Witness what Colonel Hawker says: "For a 16-bore take a shot charger that will hold 1¾oz. of shot; fill this bumper-full, and then proceed to regulate your flask and belt according to this" (I quote from memory). This would give nearly a dram over 1 1/8 oz. of shot. And the powder, from which he says "first prime", would amount to just about 3¾drams; a pretty good "whop" to put into a 16-bore of any weight, and the Colonel must have been a wonderful man to stand behind such a load throughout a good and long day's shooting.

How interesting it would be if we could know whether this was the load "old Joe" really turned out with the gun. If it were so, in the light of present knowledge, we should be almost inclined to think that old Joe Manton knew better how to charge his customers than he did his guns! What modern 12 breech-loader would stand such a load for long? But even when I began to shoot, a load for my single 14 was 2 drams of powder and 1½oz. of shot. This gun had one of Joe's last improvements. It was a self-priming flint gun, which saved a lot of trouble, as you had merely to brush out the pan, wipe the edge of the flint, and close the hammer over. On putting down the wadding over the powder, the air, passing out through the touch hole, carried enough of the powder with it to fill the pan, and miss-fires were much less frequent.

It was always the custom at my father's house to put every gun in the establishment through a thorough trial, in the early part of August, to see that none had gone off their shooting; and I, as a boy, eagerly watched these proceedings, though not allowed to take any part in them. They were conducted by my brother (eight years my senior) and Sam Wood, the old gamekeeper, with, oftentimes, a cousin of my father's, who almost always shot with him. On looking back to these trials, I must say, they were carried on in a somewhat slipshod manner. The target was put up in the shooting range, and all shots were fired at 40 yards. The load was often not marked on the sheet of brown paper shot at, thus rendering it almost impossible to refer to them at a future time, if they were still to be found.

One year both my brother and cousin were prevented attending the trials and the matter was left in the hands of the gamekeeper; and he naturally came to me to assist him, and did I not go heart and soul into the matter? I had so often seen the mess that was got into on trying to refer back to old trials, that I got sheets of paper on which was written what the gun was and to whom belonging, so as to easily identify it. On this the load for each shot was entered, and also the counted number of pellets on the brown paper; with such observations after it as "good," "patchy," "thin," or whatever the sheet dictated. I believe my father was astounded when the gamekeeper laid these reports before him, and asked Sam how he came to hit on such "a capital idea." He was at once told it entirely emanated from "Master Arthur."

From this time I was always allowed to manage these trials pretty much as I liked; and I ever afterwards kept these records of every trial, improving on them from time to time, until at last I had paper specially ruled for me for this purpose; and it was this that induced me, when I first began writing for the Press, to assume the signature of "One who has Fired some 10,000 Trial Shots at Marks"; but finding this did not adequately describe the number, I soon altered it to "20,000 Shots," which I have retained ever since, although I really believe at the present time 80,000 trial shots could be nearer the truth.

April 9th 1898

SPORTING REMINISCENCES AND ANECDOTES III
BY "20,000 SHOTS"

UPON ONE OCCASION, when I was thirteen, my father was prevented from coming down on the Friday night to shoot on the following day, as usual; but, as he wanted birds, he wrote to my mother, to say I was to go out and shoot with Sam Wood. Scarce a wink of sleep did I get that night, and by the first gleam of daylight I was up, booted, and gaitered, with my gun on my knees, but nothing would induce Sam to budge until it got to nearly ten o'clock; and well do I recollect his caution.

"Now, Master Arthur, you will be careful; recollect, my orders are, to take your gun from you if you do anything dangerous or unsportsmanlike, and I should be so sorry to have to do this. Recollect, when birds rise, put your eye on the bird you mean to shoot, and never take it off it; never mind the gun, that will go right of itself; fire the instant the gun is to the shoulder, and mind you keep both eyes open, and I'll be bound that you will soon kill some birds."

Could it be possible to give better instructions than what is conveyed in the above? And although it happened quite seventy years ago, I remember it as though it were but yesterday.

I had had one or two shots, when some birds were put into the Foxborough furze field; this was a singularly round and steep field on one side, so much so, as to be difficult to walk up or down, to keep the birds the right way. We entered at the top, and, on coming to the brow of the hill, some of them rose to the keeper, and he killed his bird. Shortly after, a single bird rose to me, some distance down the hill, so that I had to shoot down at it, and struck him hard in the back, but he sailed on, with both legs hanging down, and fell just over the fence in the next field, where we soon found him, with his wings spread out. If I was still near the old country I could point out the exact spot where the bird was shot, and where it fell.

I do not remember how many shots I had that day, probably fourteen or fifteen; but I bagged two brace, and felt as proud as a peacock. I insisted upon carrying them in my own pocket, as I was anxious to show my father the identical birds that I had shot; which I did while he was having his supper, he having arrived home very late. He was greatly pleased, and said to my mother: "Mark my words, that boy will make the best shot we have ever had in the family." I went to bed, and did sleep that night.

No doubt some of my readers will wonder how it was that we all shot with single guns. It arose in this way: my father had a rooted dislike to a double barrel, as, when quite a young man, he was staying with the Marquess of Downshire, and shooting with a friend of his, when the gentleman's gun burst. I have repeatedly heard my father say that this poor fellow was left with the butt of the gun at his should, he still holding it by the hand, and was swaying backwards and forwards, when my father ran up and just saved him from falling; the rest of the gun was blown away, the barrels were found, what was left of them, with the muzzles pointing to the shooter's feet; other portions were afterwards picked up but one lock was never recovered. Fortunately his left hand had been kept well forward, and although it was terribly cut and bruised, he did not lose his fingers; the left sleeve of his jacket was ripped up, and the forearm cut. The right hand almost escaped injury, beyond bad bruises, but the nerves of this unfortunate man were so shaken that he was long confined to the castle, and, I believe, never fired a gun afterwards. My father thereupon registered a vow never to use a double barrel, which vow he kept to his dying day; he never even liked to see them on his ground, and always used to say: "A good shot can kill quite game enough in a day, with one barrel, and a bad shot cannot use two." In consequence of this I never used a double gun until I was five or six and twenty.

Having referred to the Marquess's place I may as well tell a story often repeated to me by my two oldest aunts. During the Irish rebellion they were staying with my grandfather at Down Castle – he at that time held a captain's commission in the Downshire Yeomanry, and was, I believe, away with his troop, which had been called out, but a picquet of twenty-five men, under the command of a Captain Manley, were placed by Government in the castle for its protection. One night they were all aroused by the most fearful groans, moans, and shrieks; every creature in the castle heard them, and Captain Manley, who imagined that some poor fellow had been caught by the rebels, and was being murdered somewhere in the park, turned out the guard, who proceeded with lanterns to search everywhere, but nothing could be found. The old servants were nearly frightened to death, and kept exclaiming, "The banshee!" "The banshee!" A few days later brought the news that some member of the family had died that night, at the very hour the banshee was heard. From the description given by my aunts this visitation must have been weird and frightful in the extreme.

In the May succeeding my fourteenth birthday came one of the most remarkable events in my sporting career. Our next neighbour – about a quarter of a mile off (lived in a fine old Elizabethan house, the hall of which was glorious), and who was always known as "the squire," in riding past the keeper's cottage saw me, and beckoned me to him. After shaking hands, he said,

"Arthur, I am going to give up shooting." I immediately replied, "I am sorry to hear that," as it flashed through my mind that he would let the shooting and we should lose it, as my father had permission to shoot over the property occasionally when the squire himself was not going out. He followed it up by saying, "You know, like my uncle – your godfather – I was always a wretchedly bad shot. Now I mean to give it up to you, upon one condition – that you keep me at all times supplied with the game I require. But it must be for your own shooting; you are not to get your father or brother to help you. I don't mean that they are not to shoot over the ground, but you are to kill the game for me. Now talk to your father when he comes down on Saturday, and get his consent," adding jokingly, "I shall call you my gamekeeper, and expect to see you looking after the game. You will always have the assistance of Sam Wood, and you can have one or two of my men whenever wanted."

Fancy the joy of a boy of my age having an estate of some six or seven hundred acres, with four beautiful covers, a furze field, and a plantation of fir trees upon it well stocked with game, placed at his disposal in this manner! I rushed over to our house to tell my mother. I hardly know how I got there, but I know I was almost afraid to tell my father, and, on saying so, she said, "Never mind, leave that to me; I'll make it all right."

After breakfast on the Sunday morning, my father said to me, "Arthur, what's all this I hear about the squire's giving up his shooting to you?" I saw at a glance that it was all right, and he added, "Well, if you are going to shoot regularly you must have a certificate; I'll tell Sam to take one for you when he gets the others. Now come along with me, I am going over to the lodge to choose a brace of puppies."

We met my brother there, and they were some time making their choice, which ultimately fell on a brace of lemon and white, and then, turning to me, my father said, "I am not going to have you spoiling my dogs, so choose a brace for yourself, a dog and a slut, and then Sam can dispose of the others."

I was not long making my choice. I had often before had my eye on what Sam and I both considered the most promising pups; they were both liver and white, the white part spotted with colour, and the liver part with white.

On my meeting Sam afterwards, he remarked to me slyly, "Master seemed took with the lemon coloured ones, but I am blest if I don't think you have got the best two pups of the whole lot."

Afterwards, I was told I must break and train these pups myself my own way, as the keeper would have enough to do with the others. They were about old enough to begin, so I set to work next morning. Some weeks later my father was talking to Sam about the game, adding, "of course, you must look after the squire's ground, as that boy is not old enough to do so, and it is a beautiful beat, and so near home, I should always like to see a good head of game on it." He was told that I often helped in looking over the coverts, and that I never hardly missed a wire, and that for trapping, he (the keeper) would "back" me against any boy of my age in the county.

The fact is that at this time I had two great allies, one being an old fellow of near ninety, bent double, and hobbling on two sticks. He was called Bell, and had the credit of having been the greatest poacher in the parish. This old fellow would sit by my side on a back or stile and put me up to all the dodges of the poachers. One thing he told me struck me particularly, that was, the method of his gang in netting partridges. They used short nets, and would "cluck" the birds; and, having found out by daylight where the birds "jugged," would approach them cautiously at night until the old cock challenged by going "cluck, cluck," "cluck, cluck." The net having been previously folded together, one man carrying the half of it under his right arm, and the other man the other half under his left arm. On "clucking," the birds each would move steadily to the right and left until they got to the end of the drag ropes. When the twitch of one man was returned by the other, they both rushed rapidly forward until they heard the flutter of the birds, then the ropes were instantly dropped and the covey secured; he told me how to place the bushes so as to best circumvent this.

Subsequently they used much longer nets, but these were too heavy and "sagged" too much in the middle to be worked by hand; so the gang used to take the horses out of the farmer's stables (doubtless with the connivance of the carters). Old Bell steadily refused to do this, as horse stealing was at that time a hanging offence, and he said nobody would believe that the horses were only taken for the other work. He ultimately left the gang in consequence (but I believe it was only to form one of his own). Anyhow, the gang were caught some time after, and the leader had a very narrow escape of "a swinging." He and another, however, got off with transportation.

My other ally was "Jemmy Gent," a small farmer and butcher. Riding every day all over the parish, and often beyond, he was a splendid ally, and never failed to convey to us every bit of information as to the poaching fraternity that he could pick up on his rounds. He was very fond of me, and when I was a child and allowed to ride about the lanes on my pony, he would challenge me to race him – of course, taking care never to get before me; until one day I thought he was getting too near, and let in the whip rather sharply; and in an instant I was pitched over the pony's off shoulder. Jemmy dropped his basket, and was off his horse directly; he picked me up, and, finding I was not hurt, put me on my pony again, and from that time never challenged me to race. I shall have occasion to refer to both these worthies many times again.

Time wore on, and I had my puppies in capital order, and at last September came, and the squire said he should like to have five brace of birds, a hare, and a couple of rabbits – a pretty "big order" for a lad of "fourteen off." However, I bagged them. My readers can imagine what a happy day it was for me. My dogs behaved splendidly, and a few days later my father, who had them for a day (but hunted by myself) asked me "how the devil" I had learned to train dogs like that? He believed they were better, he said, than those turned out by Sam Wood. The truth was, I could give more time to them, as, during the whole summer, every moment that I could snatch from my private tutor was devoted to looking after the squire's ground and training my dogs.

About this time we had rather a remarkable case of what might almost be called gentlemanly poaching! Twice a year there came round our part of the world a commercial traveller, who was a terror to all the gamekeepers for miles round. He travelled in a gig; the back of the seat on the off side was so much raised that he could sit and drive almost as if he were in an armchair. He drove a capital horse, and always drove up and down hill at the same steady pace, a sort of ambling gallop, so that when he leant back it was almost like sitting in a rocking chair; hence he was known about the country as "the galloping bagman." His samples were always stowed away in boxes under the seat. He always carried a profusion of cloaks and wraps, the reason for which will appear farther on. He was on capital terms with both his horse and his dog, either of which understood him and followed the slightest word or direction. The dog was a moderate sized one, a sort of ill-bred lurcher, but quite big enough to carry a hare easily; and a knowing card he was.

This fellow was an abominable poacher, and carried with him a short double gun, the barrels being about 20in.; and he was, no doubt, a capital shot. It was supposed that one of his travelling boxes was kept solely for the gun and the game he purloined. His plan was to always leave the house he put up at very early, before anyone was about. When he got clear of the inn or village, he would put his gun together and conceal it under his multitude of wraps. If he passed a likely looking field, or saw game out feeding, he would sneak in, get a shot or two, and then bolt back to his gig. His dog (which always kept at heel) would rush in, retrieve the game, and carry it to his master. He would take one from the dog as he ran, and the dog would then go for the other. His horse always remained where he left him, and would wait any length of time; but the instant his master got his foot on the step and called out, "Go on," away the horse would go at his usual hand gallop, while the bagman would lean over the side and take the other bird from the dog, throw a cloak over the muzzles of the gun, and go along, looking as innocent as milk.

It will readily be seen how very difficult it was to catch him; he certainly had many narrow escapes, once by our own keeper, who caught him "making a mistake" and shooting a brace of pheasants out feeding on Sept. 29; he had all but got his hand on him, when the bagman called out the usual "go on," and he slipped out of his very grasp. When he got 150 yards off or so, he turned round in his seat and, in the words of dear old Thomas Ingoldsby, "placed his thumb beneath his nose and spread his fingers out," which riled old Sam above a bit; but he got clear off, and although we offered a reward to the ostler of the inn to give us notice when he next arrived (which he did), when Sam got there between four and five in the morning the bird had flown, and no one knew at what hour he had left; but he had paid his bill over night.

This poaching went on for three or four years, but at last he was fairly caught. He played his little game just on the outside of a shooting near Horsted Keynes, known as Shovelstrode (in the neighbourhood always pronounced "Showster") Woods. Winch, the gamekeeper there at the time, had been early that morning visiting a neighbouring keeper, and, as good luck would have it, stepped over the fence into the main road, nearly opposite the bagman's gig. In a moment he set down his gun and ran round it (the gig), and got through the gap, and concealed himself in the bushes, so that he could see all that went on. There was our friend, rapidly walking the field, dog at heel, he soon walked up a covey of birds, "bang bang," went the bagman, and down came a brace of birds; he turned and ran for the gap instantly, but the dog brought him a bird and galloped back for the other, just before his master reached the fence, but gave a growl which alarmed the bagman. He gave a hasty glance round, and, seeing no one, made a precipitate bolt for the gap, right into Winch's arms, and he being a fine stalwart fellow, over six feet high, brave and strong as a lion, the bagman might as well have tried to get out of a blacksmith's leg-vice as escape from his grip. "Not so fast, my friend," said the keeper, "I have got you this time on my master's ground; I must have your name and address before I let you go." "I will see you," well, we will say "jolly well hanged first," was the reply. "Well," said Winch, still holding on, "I shall have your gun and the birds, anyhow." The bagman seemed inclined to close with him; "you had better not try that game," said Winch, but he called out, "seize him, Grip," and the dog went for Winch's leg, but a kick from the keeper's heavy boot, under the jaw, sent him howling for a yard or two into the field. Winch then proceeded to get one of the birds out of the poacher's pocket and transferred it to his own; they had a scuffle, during which they both went over the gap and rolled into the ditch, but the gun fell under them, the barrels got bent considerably, and the stock was broken at the hand, the butt hanging only by the screw, through the long strap of the trigger guard.

While they were rolling, Winch got possession of the other bird. They both now scrambled up, Winch still holding on to the other's coat. He then struck Winch in the face. Winch partially let go, and the dog now returned to the charge, seizing him by the leg, but could not get his teeth through the strong leather gaiter, and the unhappy bagman received a smasher on the nose, which knocked him against the wheel of the gig, and in an instant his foot was on the step, and he called out the customary "go on," and, like a flash of lightning, was out of the reach of the keeper, much to Winch's disgust. Every effort was made to trace the rascal, but for some time without success, when, after a bit, a clue was found, through the gun; it had some maker's name in Lewes upon it, and, in consequence, of this, my gentleman was traced, and a strong letter written to his employers. Whether he was dismissed, or placed on another district, or whether he was prosecuted, I do not recollect, but it is certain that from this time "the galloping bagman" was never again seen in that part of Sussex.

Poor Winch was the victim of a careless accident. He was a very good, honest fellow, and was a great friend of our old keeper Sam Wood, who had lived as a young fellow with my grandfather. They used to assist each other, not only in giving information of poaching proceedings, but often helped each other of a night, and I was several times out with them. He was accidentally shot through both thighs, in a cottage, where a rabbiting party were having their lunch, one of the shooters, without taking the cap off his gun, laid it across his knees, and from some cause the gun exploded, with the result above alluded to. He lingered on for some time, but ultimately died of the wounds.

April 16th 1898

SPORTING REMINISCENCES AND ANECDOTES IV
BY "20,000 SHOTS"

IN THE FOLLOWING SPRING I made my first acquaintance with that most charming and fascinating sport – fly fishing. And from that time down to the present day I have been one of its most devoted followers. My father went into Devon with leave to fish some of its best rivers, and he sent for me to join him. He was himself a most accomplished fisherman. He had been educated at Blundell's School, Tiverton, and, having part of the Exe and the Loman always open to the boys, he had taken to the fly rod early. Under his practical tuition I was soon able to get a basket of trout for myself, and for long years since I have enjoyed many a splendid day's sport on the bright and sparkling rivers of Devonshire, sometimes quite filling my creel, and extending to over fifty brace, although I have returned all unsizable fish.

What an extraordinary thing is the tendency of all young fly-fishers to cram their books with every imaginable kind of fly. I did it myself when I began. In later years, as an old hand, I declare I have been so thoroughly puzzled when asked by a man on the river bank if I could recommend a fly, that, after looking through his book, I have taken one from my own, so bewildering were the numbers and colours in his.

A vast deal has been written on the subject of flies, as to whether they should be fancy or good imitations of the natural fly on the water. I have no hesitation in saying, after my long experience, that I have no faith in fancy flies. What is known as the Wickham – a blue with a bright silver body – is the only one I could ever do much with for trout. Still I do not use many flies; some thirteen or fourteen only have carried me through many seasons most successfully. As it assists some of my readers, I will here add the names of the flies, how made, and their season. At all events I have been able to kill with these flies in a number of rivers in England, Scotland, and Wales.

1. BULLOCK HAIR.- Body, made from dark red bullock hair that has been turned to a bronze-mulberry colour in the vitriol and lime pits of a tanyard (it is always to be found in a bag of builder's hair), ribbed with fine gold wire; hackle, a furnace, *i.e.,* deep red with black list up the middle, black tips to the fibre. Best season, from the earliest to the middle of March; after this up to about eleven o'clock, but may be used effectively as a stretcher throughout the whole season.
2. COLD BLUE.- Body, one half hare's ear flick, the other half house rat fur, thoroughly mixed, dressed rough; ribbed, straw-coloured silk; hackle, dark grizzled, spangled to match.
3. BLUE UPRIGHT.- Body, floss silk of an olive green, but which turns a dark slatey blue when soaked; ribbed, fine white silk; hackle, bronzey blue, which nearly matches silk when dry. For stretcher, or for tail fly. From about March 20 to middle of April, and is a fine killer. May be winged with dark, old starling wing; enlarged, and ribbed silver wire; it makes a good lake fly.
4. MARCH BROWN.- Body, three strands of mottled brown turkey-wing feather, spun on typing silk, ribbed with a

strip from a turkey quill; hackle, dark grizzled, brownish grey; always for dropper.

5. TURMERIC FLY.- Body, hare's flick, from a skin that has been dyed yellow by simmering for an hour or so in a strong solution of turmeric, with a little bit of alum added to set the colour; dry shave the back with sharp razor, by which means you only get the yellow-brown tips; dub the body with this rather rough. Ribbed, gold wire conspicuously; hackle, a rich cream colour, with black metallic list down the middle. To be used in full-coloured water when spate has just cleared enough to begin fishing, at which time it is incomparable, all the best fish taking it. May be used at all such times, and, dressed small, will often kill well in fine water and hot weather.

6. SILK TAIL.- Body, at the end, half fawn-coloured floss silk, the upper half hare's ear; hackle, a deep brick-dusty red. Makes a capital dropper in floods over No. 5.

7. HERON BLUE.- Body, three strands of heron wing feather, spun on tying silk; hackle, blue dun to exactly match. A good fly from April throughout.

8. SMOKY DUN.- Body, a sort of pale dirty orange, yellow worsted, the shade is often to be found in an old Turkey carpet; hackle, a brownish smoke-coloured dun, rather pale. From April throughout.

9. THE BUG.- Body, water rat fur; hackle, a deep blood red. An excellent fly in hot weather.

10. WHITE BODY AND RED.- Body, white floss silk, rather fine; ribbed, fine silk dark crimson; hackle, brick dust red. An excellent fly for warm weather, especially good for grayling.

11. WICKHAM.- Body, flat burnished silver; hackle, pale blue, wings to match. A fancy fly, but an excellent killer in bright water.

12. QUILL GNAT.- The ordinary fly of the shops. From middle of March throughout.
13. PALL BLUE AND SILVER.*- Again the ordinary shop fly. An excellent fly for warm weather.
14. BLACK GNAT.- Body, same floss silk as No. 3, dressed fine at end, swelling rather rapidly; no hackle. Wings, dark old starling. End of May and June.
15. SPINNER.- Body, the same as No. 2. Wings, young starling wing feather, tied dry. Dressed rather small. No better fly in fine water throughout season, especially on the Wandle.
16. TEAL WING.- A shop fly. Body, drabby, pale brown worsted. Hackle, read or black. Wings, from teal wing, with white tip. A fancy fly, but an excellent killer all the summer, from dusk to dark.

It may be thought I have not been sufficiently precise with regard to seasons. I have done this purposely, as they vary so much from year to year, even on the same river; and on others it is much more marked. For instance, I have seen the March brown, on some of the early Devonshire rivers, come on during the first few days in March; whereas, in a little stream I fished for several years in Surrey, it never appeared till about April 20, and in one year it was May before it made its appearance. But a fly fisher can never do wrong in beginning with the Bullock Hair and Cold Blue all the time the days keep cold, following sharp, white frosts; then use the Blue Upright and March Brown as directed in my list. By the middle of May much greater quantities of flies will be "on," and of different kinds, and an angler will have no difficulty in "spotting" what they are, and select a fly of the right colour and size from the foregoing list. I like some of

---

* Presumably this is an error and should read TEAL, BLUE AND SILVER.

these tied in two sizes; and have found them perfectly successful wherever I have fished in England, Scotland, and Wales (in a great number of rivers), and can safely recommend them to the consideration of my brother sportsmen.

With regard to hackle or winged flies, both are equally good, and wanted in their proper places. For a sparkling, rapid, rough trout stream, abounding in runs, sharps, and stickles, there is nothing like a hackle fly; a winged fly in such waters washes down into a lump the colour of a fly, but loses all form and shape, and consequently its attraction, whereas a hackle fly, if made from the feathers of a cock's neck, not less than three years old, always keeps its shape, partially at least, and when "touched" in working them, the fibres open and shut, giving an appearance of life, which can never be imparted to a winged fly in such a situation. But, where the river is slow, with large glassy pools, then, the winged flies are most successful, and the dry fly fishing comes in, and a fisherman cannot be considered a master of his art, unless he can properly manage both methods.

The wings of flies intended for this style of fishing should always be tied dry, and stand distinct and separate. By the way, never go dry fly-fishing without putting the Vaseline bottle in your pocket. Before commencing, dip the tip of your finger in the bottle, and enough Vaseline will adhere to it; spread this over the finger and thumb, then, holding the fly at the head, anoint it all over, taking special care not to disturb the form and position of the wings, and mind not, on any account, to get any of the Vaseline on the gut attached to the fly, as, if so, it will "bell" in the water and be shown plainly to the fish. This anointing will keep your fly mostly on the surface for an hour or more, and prevent the necessity for violently switching the fly three or four times backwards and forwards to dry it before letting it drop on the water, which invariably after a bit spoils the make and shape of the fly, the wings being broken up and muddled.

For dry fly-fishing I think it a mistake to use two flies, as it is difficult to keep both afloat, and if the drop fly goes under, from its catching the water, it soon drags the tail fly down also, much more quickly than it would without it. The great thing is to let the fly float down with the current without being dragged under. The fewer casts you can make with the dry fly the batter; never touch or lift it so long as it floats down in the proper channel.

April 23rd 1898

SPORTING REMINISCENCES AND ANECDOTES V
BY "20,000 SHOTS"

WITH REGARD TO the number of flies on the collar; when I began I used four, but I soon reduced the number to three, and for many years have only used two. I am satisfied that a moderately good fisherman will get quite as many "basketable" fish with these as with more. For many years I was acquainted with the late rector of Hawkridge, Devon; he had a capital section of fishing on the river Barle. I have seen him at work frequently, and he was a good performer; but he always had a drop fly at every knot on his collar – eight or nine of them, and when on the opposite bank, I have seen the fish come up and look at this array, and go down again. I feel certain he would have caught more and better fish had he used only two or three flies. The fact is, that these flies falling on the water like the "four and twenty fiddlers all in a row," some to the right of them, some to the left of them, and some on the top of them, scared the fish rather than induced them to rise; and they slunk off and sulked at the bottom.

In putting up a collar I think it much the best to always have your drop fly a blue of some kind, suitable to the water and weather; the only exceptions occurring to me at this moment being the March Brown and Silk Tail mentioned in a previous article. As from their position (particularly in a sharp stream) in working the flies keep bobbing about and disporting themselves exactly in the way that you see the blue flies do in these situations; and when worked in this way it has the effect of sinking the tail fly, and imparting to it the opening and shutting motion before referred to, so that you show both flies to the fish, exactly in the manner which renders them most attractive.

Some of my readers will probably remark, that some of the most well known flies are omitted from the list I have given; my reason for this is that I wish to confine my catalogue to flies of general application. Local or special flies can always be added at the discretion of the angler; many such flies are not only local, but uncertain. Take, for instance, the Grannom on the Test; at times this will take extremely well, and at others, will hardly be looked at. I fished the Test for several days on one occasion with the owner of the water; he always used the Grannom, while I stuck to my own flies, using mostly "Bullock Hair" as the tail, and I took more fish than he did.

On my introduction to this celebrated river, I was told that a fish was never to be taken with a sunk fly; but from the look of the water, I thought there must be some mistake in this, and though offered the run of my friend's book, I preferred trying my own flies. The result was that in seven or eight days I caught between eighty and ninety trout and grayling, and though the "basketable" size was set at about two pounds (a pretty stiff limit I thought), eight of my fish were voted "killable." None of them were weighed, but I think that one or two would have exceeded the prescribed weight.

Again, in the case of the May-fly (with which the best sport is obtained on the Itchen), this is a local fly. Though found on most of the Midland rivers, I have never yet seen one in Devonshire, and I have been told that they are almost equally absent on the Scottish and Welsh waters. It is doubtless a very killing fly, but, at the same time, a very difficult one. I omitted it from my list, principally because these flies, if once shut up in a book, and pressed flat, are pretty certain to be utterly ruined. They should always be carried in a box, which is a nuisance if they are not wanted.

The drakes of the present day, as turned out by the professors of fly-tying, are positive works of art, too beautiful to be spoilt by squeezing them up in a book. The Vaseline process greatly facilitates their use; but I would suggest to the angler the advantage of taking a pair of fine-pointed and very sharp scissors, and cutting off closely every fibre of the hackle pointing at all downwards, leaving only those that are horizontal when the fly is held upright, as, when the fly drops on the water, from gravitation, it naturally falls with the bend of the hook downwards. When the downward fibres are left, they catch the water and pitch the fly to the right or left as they predominate, at times causing it to lie flat on the side; whereas, when they are cut, the fibres float on the surface and keep the fly upright, just on the same principal as the oars of a boat when left in the row-locks, with the blades floating, tend to keep the boat steady and upright. I ought to have stated that this fly is so little known in Devonshire that it is a common thing among local anglers to refer to the Cannon or Downhill fly as the May-fly, and this is often very misleading to strangers visiting these rivers.

I must say that I have no faith or confidence in what are known as fancy flies. I have often tried them, and found them "wanting," unless they have happened to be a good imitation of some fly to be found on the water. Take, for instance, Holland's Fancy, that made a "sputter" some forty or fifty years ago; it is simply a good dressing of the August dun, and is an excellent killer, but I have found that the ordinary March Brown, No. 4, if dressed small, does duty for this fly exceedingly well, and the August dun is therefore omitted; in fact, during the summer and autumn many flies come on the river, so much resembling the spring flies that they may be always used for them, though in some cases a smaller size is desirable to suit the fine low water. But I am convinced that most fancy flies are almost useless; and yet I have two of them in my list, the only ones I have ever found really effective, namely, the Wickham, which I believe the fish run at, more on account of his bright shining body, which they probably take for a very small fish (a sort of whitebait *bonne bouche* to a trout) rather than a fly – at any rate, it is at times a most killing lure, whatever it may be taken for. The other is the Teal Wing. The attraction here, I think, is the large white spot on the tip of the feather of the wing, which shows and attracts the trout in the twilight. My personal experience of over sixty years (for I still am able to go on fishing) has convinced me that the more the flies on your line are a close imitation of those actually on the water the better will be the sport. Particularly, the bodies should be an exact imitation in size and colour, the wings and hackles I do not think of nearly so much consequence.

One of the great defects to be dreaded in shop bought flies is that although you send a fly to be copied, and state what the material should be, time is so precious to the people working for the shops that they will not lose it by hunting up the proper stuff, but take the first fur or worsted which is the same colour. This leads to great disappointment, as, when wet, the bodies alter in colour, or do not reflect the proper shades when in the water to match the hackle or wings. Hence the best flies may get tabooed unjustly.

I once tried a fancy fly of my own for grayling; it was made thus: body, brightest metallic green peacock herl, from an outside tail feather; tag from the brilliant crimson of the green woodpecker's topknot, from the eighth of an inch long, and dressed rather bushy; hackle, dark blue or grizzled. It killed very well in the Derbyshire waters, but finding the Bullock Hair and some other of the flies in my list equally good, I have not made it for the last thirty years or so.

In order to show that I am not giving my list of flies their sufficient grounds, I may state here that I fished for twenty seasons with a gentleman, Mr. T. Boulton (who, many years ago, married a cousin of mine). He was "out and out," the finest fly fisher for trout, and the best judge of flies I ever met with, and was most probably never equalled. We used to go away together for about four to six weeks in the spring, and again for about a month in the autumn. We never used anything but the artificial fly, and it was our custom always to return to the river all unseasonable or unsizeable fish. We kept a record of the fish actually killed by each of us. Before he left England, I, at his request, took to him all the old lists, and we totalled up the whole twenty years' sport, and found that, including salmon, sea trout, sewin, trout, and grayling, we had killed upwards of five thousand brace together. Now, I think, considering the short time we fished in each year (as he could not always get away from business), this must be almost a record score for any two men; and this was done, so far as I am concerned (except with regard to salmon), with the flies, contained in the list I have given. It is possible he may have used a few flies in addition, but we generally fished with the same.

The last trip we had together we fished the river Exe between Tiverton and Dulverton for twelve days only, and our kill was 697 trout – grand sport! It is remarkable that during all these years our kill always bore, within a fraction, the same proportion to each other, he killing three fish to my two.

I have not seen this dear old friend for upwards of ten years; he was not only the best fisherman, but the best companion I ever met in my life – genial and good tempered and always ready for a joke, or a laugh at the river side, and most liberal in supplying flies to any less successful anglers we might meet. I am delighted to say he has now returned to England, and, although hundreds of miles from me, I am looking forward with the greatest possible pleasure to our again meeting, and talking over those old happy days together.

I must now touch upon a much more difficult subject than trout – namely salmon. These fish are unquestionably the most uncertain and capricious I have ever had anything to do with. What they take the flies for is a mystery beyond me, for they certainly are like nothing "on earth, or the waters under the earth," but I fancy that they must rise out of pure "cussedness" in seeing something gaudy in colours, with a semblance of life, dragged over them. So it is well to be provided with a good stock of varied salmon flies; but, as far as I know, it is impossible to tell what they may rise at, from one day to another. At one time, when fishing the Dovey, the only fly they would look at was a Jock Scott. The next time I visited the same river, I was, of course, well provided with these flies, but not a rise could I get to one, and, at that time, the Black Doctor was in fashion, and just so it has been on all the salmon rivers I have fished.

I may mention that there is an immense advantage to a wader in carrying a wading stick; it has saved me many a ducking; to get your head under water, on a cold March day, after a sharp white frost, is by no means agreeable. Besides, prudence entails an immediate return home to obtain dry clothes. The wading stick should be strong but not thick, provided with a ferrule of about an inch of solid steel, rounded at the end like the small end of an egg; this gives a good hold on any bottom, and should be "file" hardened, as this keeps the stick always down. It should be of such a length that, when held upright by the hand in water, without wetting the hand, it will show the depth to which you can go, without getting over the top of stockings. It should be bored a few inches from the top, so as to attach it by a lanyard to the strap of the creel; on having to use the short landing net, you simply let go the stick; the heavy ferrule will not allow it to move on the bottom, and is easily recovered by the lanyard, when you have killed and basketed your fish.

Of course, at my great age, I am not so firm on my pins as I used to be, and without this third leg could not venture to wade at all; the top of my stick, which is made of pimento wood, has a very acute hook, which I have found most useful in pulling down boughs, to clear a collar that has become hitched up.

I have always been afraid of wading trousers, when strapped round the waist, they confine a lot of air, and, in case of slipping, or losing your balance in deep water, would inevitably keep the lower extremities up, and the head under water, with even a strong swimmer. Consequently, I have never worn them. Some years ago I lost a very dear friend in this manner; he was Mr. Fyfe, a gentleman very high up in the Post Office, one of the nicest fellows possible; he was a great salmon fisher, and always spent his vacation in Scotland for this purpose. One day he was looking over some of my flies and tackle, when I showed him some of my peculiar salmon casts; they were made in this way; three distinct collars were made up of about ten feet long, carefully tied, tapered, and tested; they were then laid side by side to see that no two knots were less than about three inches apart; if they were so a length was taken out and a longer or shorter one substituted, as required. These were twisted together for the entire length; this I managed by placing the spinner on the staircase, so as to get length enough for the heavy weight at the bottom; by this means any large knot in the collar or whippings are entirely avoided. Mr. Fyfe was immensely pleased with these, and asked me to make some for him, and always after came to me to make them. On his last trip, poor fellow, he came as usual, telling me he had never once broken with one of my collars, but that he had given several away to friends in Scotland, and so wanted more. I took them to him just that morning, telling him there were more and better fish up the river than usual, but alas! I never saw him again. I heard soon afterwards that he had been drowned. The sad story that reached me later on was this: He had crossed the river twice at one spot during the day safely, but, as the river was higher than usual, the water was nearly up to the top of his trousers. On crossing at the same place for the third time, a puff of wind carried his hat off, and in endeavouring to clutch it he lost his balance, and was immediately carried into deep water, when these wretched trousers kept his legs up and his head under; he was, of course, soon drowned. His body was recovered the next day some distance down the river, still floating in the manner described. This horrible event confirmed my dislike of wading trousers.

The stockings, being open at the top, instantly fill with water, and, though very heavy to move, as they do not admit of very deep wading, there is no fear of drowning, should you unluckily get capsized.

April 30th 1898

SPORTING REMINISCENCES AND ANECDOTES VI
BY "20,000 SHOTS"

I WENT AWAY FLY FISHING with my dear old father when I was about fifteen, so I must get back to about the same period. I now began to institute a number of gun trials on my "own hook," to try and find out better results from loading, which I took care should be duly chronicled. I rather think he fancied I was wasting a lot of ammunition and brown paper – which, of course, he had to pay for; but he put no restriction upon me, and when I could show him (which I did shortly) a considerable improvement in the shooting of one of his guns, it was at once all right.

On the 1st of September of that year my brother and a friend went off with the gamekeeper, and I went out with my father. He had been very much overworked in business at this time, and I know as a fact that he had not had a gun in his hand since the 20th of the previous October; yet he never missed a shot all day. Having been overworked and not very well, he could only stand a short day, so he went over *my* ground close round the house, and he had my brace of dogs. We did not start till past ten, and were home again soon after three, having gone in for nearly an hour for lunch and a rest; but he had seventeen shots, and I carried in for him eight brace of birds and a landrail. What I did myself on that particular day I do not distinctly remember;

but he was delighted with my dogs, and as we had a way of our own in breaking dogs, I think it will not be amiss to give a short account of it here.

We had a walled garden at the house, about fifty yards by twenty; the walks were lined with espalier fruit trees, and the beds well stocked, so that there was always admirable covert. In this we kept a pinioned cock pheasant and a partridge, a hare and a rabbit, and here we did all the breaking, save teaching the pups how to quarter their ground. Each pupil was taken in daily alone, for about a quarter of an hour, and everything was taught by kindness and rewards. The first thing to be done (not in the walled garden) was to have the pup toddling about after you playing with and talking to him, until you have secured his affection; and not till then were the puppies introduced to the game.

I used to begin with them at about four or five months, and in a few weeks had them sufficiently in hand for the garden. My instruments of torture consisted of three suckers from the nut bushes – about the size of the stem of a tobacco pipe and fifteen or sixteen inches long. It was seldom indeed that I ever broke even one of these over the back of a puppy. On the other hand, for rewards, I used to get the cook to boil a piece of liver, mince it up fine, and mix it with a little quite plain paste, and boil it like a roly-poly pudding. A slice of this was cut off, and cut into squares about the size of dice; these were carried in a paper bag in my pocket; whenever the pups did well in "finding and standing" the game they were rewarded with a bit of pudding, and if specially well, two or three. It was astonishing how rapidly they would learn their work under this judicious treatment. Thus a little over an hour a day would train four puppies in "the way they should go." Beating the fields was afterwards taught by taking them out singly with a very steady old dog, and subsequently in pairs without him – always the brace that were intended to be hunted together. By this simple means were taught some of the finest dogs I have ever seen. It was often the cause of much fun, later on, to many of our friends, when the dog ordered to retrieve, on bringing me the bird, looked up into my face and plainly asked for his bit of pudding; as he would know as well as I did when he had done well. I generally had the pudding in my pocket to reward him.

As far as my experience of professional dog-breakers goes, I would not trust a valuable whelp to many of them. I believe them to be for the most part unthinking and cruel, never considering that the chief difficulty in teaching a dog is to make him understand what you want him to do, and your puppy is generally only too willing and anxious to do it. I remember once astonishing one of these fellows, and stopping his unmercifully thrashing a young dog, by asking him if he understood Italian or French. On his answering "No," I said, "Suppose I gave you an order in one of these languages, and because you didn't do it, knocked you down with my stick and thrashed you till every bone ached – do you think you would have been able to comprehend what I meant any better for the thrashing? Now, that is just what you are doing with that puppy." He thereupon remarked, "Oh, I never thought of that," and looked, if possible, a bigger fool than he was.

We generally used to breed a few dogs every year, and, although I do not profess to have much experience in this, I do not like the principle of breeding "in and in." You undoubtedly gain in beauty by it, but you lose in intelligence; and the most lovely pup in the world is of no use if it is half an idiot. Handsome dogs are always to be met with of quite different breeds, and I think it much better to have new blood as often as possible. It is remarkable how clever cross-bred or half-bred dogs are. For retrievers I always got a cross-bred puppy, and I always tried them for a short time. If they did not show brains and an aptitude to learn, I consigned them at once to the pond, as it is of no use wasting time over such dogs. If the raw material is not what it should be, it is much less trouble to get another and begin again.

In choosing young pups out of a litter, there is one thing that I have always found an indication of good sense. On looking at the pups, whistle or chirrup to them and note which takes most notice. If any one of them looks up at you, wrinkles his brow, and puts his little chubby head on one side, repeat this at intervals two or three times, and if attended with the same results, do not hesitate for a moment to choose that pup, though others may be much more prettily marked. I have always found it a sure sign of intelligence.

With regard to the probable size of dogs, a good guess may be made by examining the feet and limbs – if thick and clumsy, though well shaped, the dog will be much larger than one of less make in this respect. I myself much prefer dogs of a small breed; they have not so much to carry, and consequently do not tire so soon. I think the narrow nose and light head much prettier than what used to be known as the old Spanish breed of pointers. Their powers of nose are certainly quite equal. I believe I was one of the first to stop the brutal practice of cutting off about half a pointer's tail. I argued that, as Nature gave a dog a tail, it was for some good purpose, and that cutting it only made the dog ugly.

My father had an extraordinary experience, I suppose I had better call it a coincidence, with regard to a dog. Soon after his marriage, a gentleman living in Ireland (a client of his), who had large estates in the West Indies, wrote to say that he had to visit them, and should be in London on a particular day; but that, as he should probably be absent a couple of years, he would bring over with him his favourite pointer for my father. He arrived in due course, called on my father at his office, and told him he had brought the dog "Swig" to England. My father asked him to dine with him the following day but one. Next morning he found his friend at the office waiting for him, to tell him that the ostler, in whose charge he had left the dog, had foolishly opened the stable door, when the dog rushed out and bolted from the yard, but he was doing everything he could to recover it. On my father's return home that night between nine and ten (he seldom left the office before nine o'clock) he found on his doorstep a remarkably handsome pointer. The dog rose as he approached, evidently welcoming him; and patting him on his head, my father remarked "Well, you are a splendid fellow; you will soon be inquired for; I won't turn you out."

On the door being opened, the dog walked in as though at home, and laid himself down on the hearthrug in front of the fire. The next day my father came home earlier to meet his friend, who was to dine with him. On the latter's knocking at the door, the dog bounded into the hall. In a few seconds the door was opened, and the first thing my father heard was his friend exclaiming, "By Jove, there's Swig! How did he get here? Who brought him?" He was at once told how the dog had been found. "Well," said he, "this is the most remarkable thing I ever heard of; but I am heartily glad the dear old dog has been found. He is the finest dog I ever shot over, and I should have still more regretted his loss if you had not got him, because I know he will be so well cared for."

Now, how did this dog find his way to my father's house? He had never been in London or in England before; and it was a good two miles and a half from the hotel his master put up at. Was it not a most singular coincidence that he should by chance have gone to the door of his future master?

The dog accompanied him to my grandfather's at Batness for the following first of September, where he remained for years. He at last got so old that my father had to lift him over the gates and hedges; but so good a dog was he that he always hunted for such time as his failing strength permitted. At last he died by the kitchen fire. Of course I do not recollect the dog, as it came to my father's eight or nine years before I was born, and was not a young dog when he had him first; but I have often heard my father, my mother, and an uncle tell the story of poor old "Swig."

Ordinarily, I shot a great deal with my brother, and for many years we had a standing bet of a half-crown on the first shot of the season, for the benefit of our good old keeper; yet it is a remarkable how very seldom either of us had to pay it, as we either both missed or both killed our first shot; and I think it was only twice that old Sam got his half-crown. But on one occasion my brother treated me vilely; the first field we entered was a little corner piece, not a quarter of an acre, between some woods, in which there was scarcely ever a bird to be seen; we were walking along the road through it, talking as usual when not expecting game, when two old birds rose close to us. I shot at mine but missed it in a most unaccountable manner, as it was a complete "band box" shot, and not more than five and twenty yards off. My brother then deliberately took his gun down from his own bird to shoot mine, and said quietly, "Now old boy shell out your half-crown to Sam." If this was not adding insult to injury I do not know what is.

He was a very pretty shot on the wing, but, vulgarly speaking, I could "lick his head off," boy as I was then, at ground game, and I said "I will be upsides with you before the day is out," when he replied, "All right, old fellow; but it won't cost me half a crown." And sure enough so it was; he missed a hare grandly in an open oat stubble, whereupon I bowled it over immediately. Poor old fellow! The very last time I saw him before his death he reminded me of this circumstance, and we had a good laugh over it.

One day we were having our lunch in a field, which was divided at a narrow place by posts and rails. Our guns were safely deposited against one post. I sat down with my back against the lower rail, but he preferred to perch on the next post with one leg on the bottom rail on each side of it – not altogether a very secure perch, as the sequel will show. In the middle of our lunch a little bird came and settled on the very top of a small teller oak in the spinney, a little to the right and behind him, and commenced singing "tweet, tweet, tweet," repeating this several times. My brother called out "She-w," and clapped his hands; but there the bird sat, constantly repeating "tweet, tweet, tweet," and at last my brother exclaimed, "Confound you, if you go on 'tweeting' in that way I'll shoot you." But still the little bird went on perseveringly with his "tweeting," and would not be driven off, in spite of all our laughing and talking. At length Farry said to me, "Give me my gun; I'll soon settle him." I, of course, handed it to him, and he deliberately put in the "patch," but found he had to screw himself round considerably to bring the gun to bear on the bird, making his seat on the post still more unstable; he took a most deliberate aim, and bang went the gun; at the same time old Farry (an abbreviation of his name, Farindon, my mother's maiden name) went over the post the back way, with legs and arms in the air, amidst yells of laughter from the whole party, including the prostrate one; and the lucky little bird flew over his head calling out "tweet, tweet, tweet," as he went.

I have seen many extraordinary shots, but thank God never an accident, beyond a dog or two getting peppered. One day we were shooting a little spinney (a very steep hanging bank), not twenty yards across – a very favourite place for a cock pheasant at mid-day. My father and I were standing at the top, the gamekeeper having gone in at the bottom with the beagles to hunt it along; a cock pheasant rose to my father, who shot it so directly over the keeper that as it fell he caught it in his hands as he would a cricket ball, but having fallen some fifty or sixty feet, it feel with such force that it nearly knocked him over.

We always kept nine or ten couples of beagles in hunt that were trained to the gun, and we commonly shot pheasants over them, preferring them to spaniels; they were so well broken that after being once or twice called off "flick" in the morning, they would stick to their pheasants all day, not following a hare or a rabbit more than two or three yards, but would keep working close round the guns; and most valuable little dogs they were – so much so that the keeper always got a couple of pounds for spare six-weeks' puppies after our own selection had been made. So splendidly broken were they that we could stop them at once if in full cry across the open, not three minutes behind a hare or a rabbit. If I held up my hand and called, "Away! Away! Away!" they would leave a hot scent and come circling round to my heels, and look up as much as to say, "What the deuce did you call us off for?"

I can hardly fancy anything better than this. They were beautifully bred, of two kinds, either blue mottled or lemon pied; and on showing the "cry" one day to an old fox hunter, he said, "By Jove, they are splendid," and look "just like foxhounds seen through the wrong end of an opera glass." We kept them as level as possible, and if any of them exceeded 10 lb, weight in hunting order, we draughted them out of the "cry;" as, of course, the smaller they were the easier they could get through the furzes and rough covert, and the slower they were the better for the gun.

One year Mr. Wood, the banker, then living on the "Hog's Back" near Godalming, wrote to my father to ask him if he could spare or get four or five couples of our breed and send them over to him. These were got together after a little time, among them a dog called "Tanner." He was bought from a cottager at Forest Row, about six miles from us, and was kept with the other in one of our kennels for about three weeks before the requisite number was made up, when each dog was packed in a separate hamper, and despatched by the carrier's slow waggon through the night to London. Next day they were picked up by the Godalming coach, and sent on in the same way to Mr. Wood's house. After a lapse of about a month, my father got a letter one morning, from Mr. Wood, stating that the gamekeeper had that day let the beagles out into a field for exercise, but that Tanner had bolted. It struck my father that he might have returned home, so he told Sam Wood to take the gig and drive over to Forest Row and inquire if the dog had returned. On reaching the cottage the first thing he saw was Tanner sitting at the door. He was, of course, claimed and brought home, and, after a few days, again despatch in a hamper to Mr. Wood. A few weeks later we heard that Tanner had again bolted, but on sending over to Forest Row, nothing could be heard of the dog, the former proprietor declaring on his honour that he had seen nothing of him, - though we heard afterwards that the said Tanner was as good as an annuity to his master, as he sold him every year, and sometimes twice in the year, for never less than two pounds, as he was a really very handsome dog, and was of our own breed, but too large for our "cry." Doubtless the last time we sent for him the gamekeeper had arrived too late, the people having had time to put him quietly out of the way. Now, it has often occurred to me, I should like to know how the dog got home so quickly. Did he go all the way round by London, or cut across country, which would very much shorten the distance? Truly this "homing" principle in dogs is a very mysterious thing. I shall probably have occasion to refer to this subject again in the course of these pages.

May 7th 1898

SPORTING REMINISCENCES AND ANECDOTES VII
BY "20,000 SHOTS"

REMARKABLE GUNS – POACHERS – SHOT AT A FROCK AND ITS RESULTS – MAN NEARLY SHOT

AMONG THE NUMEROUS GUNS belonging to my father were two a little out of the common track. One was the most pronounced "bell-mouthed" gun I have ever seen. It was a splendid old stub-twist barrel of "inch strap," of a most beautiful pattern, quite equal to Old Joe Manton's barrels, forged for him by Fullerd, and the whole gun was turned out in the best possible style of its time. It had belonged to my grandfather, Mr. Farindon, and was, I believe, his favourite gun. It had upon it the name of Utting in gold letters, and the pan, and touch hole, and thumbplate, were also gold.

The barrel was thirty-two or thirty-three inches long, plug-breeched. At this end it was about 13-bore; this gradually tapered for about ten inches, during which it was reduced to a 16 gauge; for the last eleven or twelve inches it gradually opened out to about 11 gauge. I am speaking from memory, as I have not seen the gun for nearly seventy years; but I know the barrel was sixteen in the middle, for I well remember that a card wad of this gauge, screwed on to the worm of the ramrod, dropped down to the first ten or eleven inches, then went quite tight until it reached the opening behind, when, after passing more easily for a couple of inches, it dropped with the weight of the rod on to the breech. Of course in such a barrel, no wadding such as was then known, could possibly be used, so the loading had to be done with brown paper.

This curious gun might have done very well in my grandfather's time, when shots were probably seldom taken at any ranges over thirty yards; but of all the "scatter guns" I ever saw, this was the widest. It may be said, perhaps, "No wonder," considering the nature of the barrel, which was a complete caricature upon "Old Joe's" boring, of "opening" behind and "relief" in front. Load it how you would, nothing even respectable could be got out of it beyond thirty yards. At that distance, with 1½oz. of shot, it made a pretty fair but a rather uncertain pattern of nearly 4ft. diameter. (It would have been a glorious gun for a bad shot at driven game in the present day.) But at forty yards there were endless spaces between the pellets of five or six inches, and I am afraid to say what the width of the pattern would have been; our 4ft. 6in. targets would certainly have not taken half of it. It was for some time the gamekeeper's gun, but on his complaining of not being able to kill vermin with it, at any reasonable distance, it was handed over to me to shoot; hence my accurate recollection of what it was.

On my father being made acquainted with its performances, he at once said, "That will never do," and the gun was given away to a farmer, who had known it in my grandfather's days. I much regret this now, as I should have been very glad to have had such a gun (which was a curiosity in its way) among my collection of old sporting arms. The maker, Utting, I believe, had his place of business in Blackman-street, Borough, and flourished towards the end of the last century.

The other gun to which I have alluded was by Ezekiel Baker, of Whitechapel. My uncle, the Major, picked it up somewhere abroad, and gave it to my father on his returning to England with his battery. This gun had Baker's improved patent breech; it was a singular construction, and now so out of date that it is worth describing. There was in the lid of the gun-case (under the name and address of the maker) a full-sized section drawing. The front of the breech was cupped out, exactly like Joe Manton's, with his ante-chamber; behind this, the breech was drilled through from side to side; then two plugs were screwed in to exactly meet in the middle, the end of each being "cherried" out to exactly a hemisphere. These were screwed in, and the ante-chamber then drilled into the circular opening, which would hold between half and three-quarters of a dram of powder. The touch-hole was drilled to come exactly in the centre of the globe. The gun certainly shot very hard, but beyond this I could see no advantage in this elaborate breech; and as for kicking – Oh! To talk of "kicking like a horse" is not in it. I should think that the kick of an elephant would more nearly represent it; and no matter how much the load might be reduced, still the kicking was there. I fancy it must have been inherent to the curious little round globe, from which the way out for the gas generated, being so narrow – only about the eighth of an inch in diameter.

Poor old Sam had this gun for a short time, but the punishment he went through was truly awful. How he got through an ordinary day's shooting with it, and be able to kill anything is still a mystery to me. His cheek, and sometimes his eye, would be blackened, while his shoulder would display all the tints of the rainbow; and, although he wrapt up the trigger guard in flannel list his middle finger was always bruised and sometimes cut. Of course he was not allowed to use this for long. He then took to an 18-bore Birmingham gun, which my brother and I bought at Dean's, in Monument Yard, for three pounds. We bought it for shooting blackbirds and thrushes flying out of the gooseberry and currant bushes; it had a 30in. barrel, shot well, and went pleasantly, and I believe old Sam stuck to it to the last.

Among my earliest ventures with double-barrelled guns was one by Sam Nock, Piccadilly-circus. I had two offered me at the same time, the price of both being nearly the same. The other was by Smith, of Princes-street; but the "Nock" was so much more handy that I took that. It was a 14 bore, but it had 30in. barrels, and this made me so much slower (though it was everything that could be desired for handiness) that I only shot a few days with it, and went back to short barrels and small bores.

Since then I have had, and shot, guns of almost every well-known maker, whether London or provincial, and have, in point of fact, spent a little fortune on guns and trial shooting, as I never refused to try a gun of any make, and for anyone who sent them to me for trial. I was thereby every season gaining experience and knowledge in the peculiarities of guns. Some seasons, I believe, I have had as many as a dozen or twenty sent to me, both by friends and by strangers, with a request that I would try them and report as to their quality and loading. This I, of course, did, at my own expense; but I never regretted it, as it gave me such excellent opportunities of acquiring information, and also the makes and borings of all the crack makers.

In the spring of 1832, I regret to say, we lost our dear mother, who had long been an invalid. Soon after this my father retired from business, gave up his town residence, and dwelt entirely in the county. At this time we had the shooting, by right of property, lease, or leave, over about 6,000 acres, and some of it capital shooting, for the days of muzzle-loaders over dogs, and all wild birds.

We had a rather amusing incident, in respect to poachers, which, however, might have led to very disagreeable consequences. Instead of sleeping at the house I preferred having a small room, which was kept for emergencies at the keeper's lodge, as it enabled me to slip out with him at night or at any time. My old ally, Jimmie Gent, had brought us the information that whenever a raid was intended, on any part of our ground, by the chief gang of poachers, one of them mounted guard in the hedgerow to see if Sam and I went out, when he at once bolted off at the "double" to inform the others.

One night, soon after this, I found old Sam sitting up for me (as I generally went in calling out who it was, locked the door, and went straight up to my bedroom), on asking what was up, he told me that Tom Knight (the dog boy) had left his smock frock hanging up in the cherry tree, so that it looked just like somebody half concealed by the body of the tree; and he suggested that I should turn out about one o'clock, open the window, call out, and then fire at the frock; so accordingly I only half undressed, and lay down on the bed, and when I judged it to be about the time, opened the window, and called out, "Who is there," and then, after a pause, adding, "If you don't answer I shall fire"; no answer coming, "bang" went the gun, and down went the smock frock, and in a few minutes we were both outside to inspect the result. Of course, finding only the frock we purposely feigned a good laugh and went into bed. On inspecting it in the morning we found the breast of it had had a pretty good "peppering"; and I said, "Well I must give Tom a new frock."

Jimmie Gent was duly informed of the proceeding the next day on his calling for orders; and, before noon, it was all over the parish, of course, with due additions in the telling, until at last it was said that I had shot a man and killed him. But the beauty of the story is to come. A few days after Jimmie came to me and said, "My eye, sir, you nearly did it t'other night. There was a man a-watching of yer, and he happened to be right in the line of the tree, laid up in the hedge. He was afraid to answer when you called out, or to move, and when you fired he thought he was shot, and some of the charge peppered his feet as he stood there, but being small shot, did not get through his strong boots. He told me he never stopped running till he got inside his cottage and examined his boots." However, the affair had one good effect. The scamps were afraid to watch us again.

MAY 14th 1898

SPORTING REMINISCENCES AND ANECDOTES VIII
BY "20,000 SHOTS"

POACHING FOR PARTRIDGES WITH TRAPS – STICK AND BASKET – PRIVATE MARKS IN THE KEEPER'S TRACKS – FISH POACHER GETTING A COLD BATH

ONE DAY OLD BELL (the retired poacher) was telling me how they used to pitch traps for catching partridges. This was a scheme I had never even dreamt of before, but I was so impressed with it that I thought I would try the experiment for myself. Accordingly I put four rat traps into my pockets and sallied forth to experiment with; but inasmuch as poachers, as well as sportsmen, may possibly read my reminiscences, I will not state the *modus operandi,* though I will go as far as this, that if any proprietor or keeper finds rabbit traps painted sand colour or the colour of the soil, let him at once look out for his partridges. I proceeded to set these traps in the manner suggested to me, and on my returning in less than an hour I was horrified at my own success, for I found an unhappy partridge caught by the legs in each trap. As they all had broken limbs, there was no releasing them, so I put the poor things out of their misery as quickly as possible. On my way home I met the keeper and told him what I had done, remarking, "I don't know what to do with the birds, as I dare not tell my father." He then suggested that I should lay them all down together and take a shot at them as they lay, and then carry them in, as if I had shot them in the ordinary way. And all went right, as it was in the middle of September.

This little adventure, however, saved us many a brace of birds, and cost the poachers sundry traps, as we knew exactly where and how to look for them. And through old Bell, as may be supposed, I picked up a pretty thorough knowledge of the ways and doings of poachers in those times; and the knowledge so acquired, has, in after life, been of the greatest service to me. It enabled me not only to look after the poachers but the keepers also, as I grieve to say I have not found them all as straightforward and honest as dear old Sam Wood.

I have frequently been asked what I thought the best way of arming keepers for a night's encounter with poachers. In those days poachers seldom carried firearms, unless they went out to shoot pheasants on the roost; their proceeding in this way I might as well relate. Six or eight of them would go together, and the captain would drop a man under each tree where a bird was seen until he alone was left to "tree his bird." On his doing so he would shoot at once; all the rest would then fire as quickly as possible, secure their birds, and bolt separately for the rendezvous.

On such an occasion guns are only in the way. My dear old father used to say: "Carry your pistols by all means, as much gunpowder and brown paper as you like, but no lead." I used to make the waddings for this purpose by ramming small pieces of brown paper (thoroughly soaked in water, with a small portion of glue in it, making a sort of size) into a brass tube a good bit larger than the bore of the pistols to allow for shrinking; the whole was rammed down tight with a loader and mallet, and placed in a slack oven. When thoroughly dry they were sawn off in lengths of about ¾in. These were driven into the barrel (of the short screw-barrel pocket pistols) with a rammer and mallet till they reached the thread, the chamber and cap of the pistol being filled with powder. Subsequently experiments were made with these, and it is lucky they never had to be used, as I believe they would have been as fatal as a bullet, for on firing at a three-quarter deal board at a distance of about 6ft. from the muzzle, the board was split and smashed up frightfully. After that a less destructive wadding was substituted, as the flash alone moderately confined seemed enough to knock a man over at close quarters.

But the most effective weapon I have ever known is a stick and basket. I must be understood, however, not by any means to intend the ash sapling usually employed for teaching the broadsword exercise; these are too liable to break short off. It should be made of some tough, strong wood. I think a piece of straight-grained yew the best. It should be planed up, out of the solid, the shape of the section of an egg through the long way, and be about an inch through at the basket, slightly tapered to the point, which should be nicely rounded off – the narrower portion to represent the cutting edge – and be about 30 inches long from basket to point. The handle should be larger, and a good inch left beyond the peg, to form a pommel to the sword. I like the hand inside the basket lapped tightly round with strong whipcord, taking care that several turns go through the basket, and over and round the pommel and peg, so as to keep the hilt always firm. The basket should be painted a dark dull grey, otherwise it will be seen a field off. A sword knot should be attached, looped round the handle and round the wrist, so as to prevent your being disarmed, and having your own weapon turned against you. This, I think, is best made in the form of a "grummet" of soft worsted cord; it will take nearly four yards to make. In the hands of a swordsman, nothing can equal this as a weapon of offence and defence. Hodge's clumsy blows, with his cudgel, are easily parried, while he is at your mercy to hit him where you like; but I should always avoid playing at the head (that is, the seventh cut). In the first place, poachers carry their wire coiled up in separate rings, wrapped up in their handkerchief, in the crown of the hat; this makes it almost as good as a helmet – and a side blow across the head and temple is dangerous. But the mighty surprise is to give point, this is so perfectly unexpected; and a thrust with a good lunge, aimed at the throat or mount, and Hodge goes over on his back "like a ninepin," especially if he get a "mouthful of stick," and will not recover himself to get up for some minutes. This enables attention to be turned to any comrade who may be hard pressed. There, a good "swipe" over the shin, will not only bring Mr. Poacher down on his nose, but probably render him *hors de combat* for three or four weeks. The grand thing is, never to forget to give point whenever an opportunity offers.

Perhaps in these days of volunteering, a poacher may also be a swordsman; but even then, you are only well, but not over matched. I always thank my dear old father for having had me made a swordsman when quite a boy; it has saved my head on several occasions.

Now, I should think a bulldog revolver, loaded with a very heavy charge of powder and a thick felt wad, on which pour a little lac varnish to stick it into the shell, would be a far better weapon than pocket pistols. But it should have a strong lanyard bound with a wax end on to the butt, and at the other end a loop, so that the line can be drawn through it; this should be placed over one shoulder and under the other arm; if merely passed round the neck, it might be clawed and pulled so tight as to strangle the wearer. This lanyard should be just long enough to go round as above, and allow the pistol to be used or placed in the pocket, and will effectively prevent its being knocked out of the hand and lost on the ground. In such an event it can be easily recovered for use by means of the lanyard.

In my time, poachers always avoided coming to close quarters, if they possibly could. Mere wires or traps they readily abandoned; but they would show fight in defence of nets (which are expensive), or if driven into a corner, so that escape was difficult. Thanks to my being a swordsman, the worse treatment I ever got was being pitched head first into some furzes; I was not hurt, but my face for a day or two had somewhat the appearance of a plum pudding. I knew my man, and consequently (in dread of a warrant) he withdrew until the matter was statute run; so we got rid of that scoundrel, for a time.

Going about our grounds, the keeper and myself had our own private walks and tracks, through hedgerows and coverts, the end of which we concealed as closely as possible, being most careful ourselves to leave no footmarks at the entrances or exits. Across these tracks we used to lay a piece of bramble, if possible carefully removing and replacing it on passing. In default of this a dark green or brown thread was tied to a bough on one side; and hung over a bough on the other side. These, of course, would be quite unnoticed by any one but ourselves, but told us, as distinctly as possible, if any one had passed since we left, as they were placed too high for a dog to touch. Such an occurrence was a signal to look round and find out what was up.

Another good dodge is to make some strong pegs about 10in. long; on these cut a groove in the top, drive a wire into a hole an inch or so below the top, bend the wire over and along the groove, and drive a staple over it into the top. Do precisely the same thing with another peg, leaving about 18in. between them; paint the top of the pegs a dull brownish green. Drive these with a good mallet into the ground on each side of your track, so that the wire will stand straight across about 3in. high. By those knowing where they are, they are easily stepped over; but a stranger catches his toe and goes a cropper forwards. These should be pretty constantly shifted; half-a-dozen and a mallet can be easily carried in a hare pocket, and no one the wiser. If anybody is unlucky enough to trip his toe and get a nasty fall, there is no difficulty in seeing all about it; the broken boughs and crushed ferns, grass, and brambles sufficiently disclose the fact. And poachers, when they have once had a personal experience of these innocent little traps, have a salutary dread of them, as it effectually prevents their cautiously creeping through a covert without leaving much trail behind them; and, if carried off or thrown aside, they are very easily and inexpensively replaced.

In one of our coverts was a small brook, which rose from two springs, one of which threw out an immense volume of water, the hole under a stone from which it rose being fully the size of a hat; and in the hottest weather this water was so cold near its source that not a frog or insect was ever to be seen in it, but there were a few little trout. My father had bays placed across this at all convenient places; in some of these the water would be 3ft. or 4ft. deep, and in these the trout grew to a good size; I have taken them 12in. or 14in. long. But the poachers soon found them out, and their *modus operandi* was to tie an iron three-pronged fork on to the end of a stick 3ft. or 4ft. long; and with this they speared any trout they could see, holding them down till they ceased kicking before lifting them out.

Old Sam, one day, walking through the covert, heard a stick crack, and instantly suspected what was up. He could creep through a covert as noiselessly as a Red Indian; he soon came upon a fellow, down on one knee, with the other leg stretched straight out behind him, peering into one of the largest of these pools. Sam set his gun down, seized the fellow by the leg, and pitched him head first into the water, holding on for some little time, until probably the gentleman (!) had swallowed more cold water than he was accustomed to or was good for him. His astonishment must have been great on finding himself, on emerging, in the grip of the gamekeeper. With chattering teeth he begged hard to be let off, but steadily refused his name, or where he came from. Wood said: "I know you – you come from Forest Row, and I shall summons you." He was then allowed to depart shivering, for a walk of six or seven miles home. Of course, his basket, fish, and spear were confiscated, and the latter was hung up in the gun room as a trophy; and he too, departed, until the offence was "statute run," so we got rid of him for a while.

May 21st 1898

SPORTING REMINISCENCES AND ANECDOTES IX
BY "20,000 SHOTS"

MY LONDON LIFE AND PLEASURES – A LIFE-LONG FRIENDSHIP – MY BROTHER'S DUCKING

IT NOW BEGAN to be time to consider what was to be done with me. I was very intimate then with a young fellow, some years my senior – the son of an old client of my father's; he was an articled pupil of the celebrated John Duffel Harding, and was getting on splendidly as a draughtsman under such able tuition. I was always passionately fond of the fine arts, and through him got some of Harding's sketches, for copying, and was overjoyed one day when I was told that Harding had seen some of my copies and expressed his willingness to take me as a pupil; so when my father was talking to me about my future, I mentioned this, and said how much I should like to become an artist. He exclaimed, "What! You an artist! Why, my dear boy, you would never make your salt. No, no, when I retired from business, it was arranged that you should be taken as an articled clerk, without a premium. It will be a capital opening, as no doubt you will eventually become a partner in the firm." So it was decreed that I should go to London and enter the legal profession.

All this was soon carried out; but oh, the change to me, after the freedom of the country, and the constant run of gun or fishing rod! However, I survived it, and here I am now, writing these reminiscences. But even at the present time I am not able to determine which I disliked most, law or London. I plodded on, and one thing was a little compensation; having good introductions, I soon made numerous acquaintances, and almost immediately received an invitation to Lord Truro's, the then Lord Chancellor. It was a big and very grand affair; and while at this and many other such gatherings I could not help thinking how much I should have preferred walking through the wild woods, with the old gamekeeper for a companion, in the lovely quiet moonlight.

With what joy, however, did I hail the "long vacation" that I might get back to the country and enjoy all my old sylvan pursuits! Alas, it was too soon over, and I had to return to that abominable London and to work. This I did pretty well until the London season again commenced; then all my old acquaintances and gaieties returned, and truth to tell, I am afraid dry law books were left on the shelves. But with all I sadly missed the resources of my brother's lathe room and tools, so I set up a little workshop of my own in the corner of my room, with a small lathe and bench; and I have no hesitation in saying it kept me out of a lot of mischief, as I could always find something to do at home. Moreover, I found a place in the Islington Fields (Copenhagen House), where there was a target and a shooting ground, and I often used to go there of a morning, to try guns and experiments, having made an arrangement with the market by which I could get into the ground, find the whitewash pail and brush, and have my shoot often before anyone was up at the tavern. These resources made London a trifle more bearable to me.

I suppose I was not a very active clerk in the office I was in; for I found I was given less and less to do. There was a gentleman's office in the establishment, where all the articled clerks were assembled, some of them being country gentlemen come up to see a year or two of London practice; and I am afraid a great deal more was said about shooting, fishing, and hunting than anything else. I only once remember a point of law being discussed. One of these gentlemen (from Wales) was a clever fellow, and, if he had known a little law, he might be said to have had a smattering of almost everything. He wrote for two or three Welsh papers; he used to amuse himself by writing these articles in the office, and then amused us by reading them aloud and having discussions upon them.

After a year or two of this, I began to see that it would not do; and we got no business at all unless there happened to be "a rush" for copies of deeds or proceedings; then, indeed, we had too much of this work, and at length some of us rebelled, and there was a row. I complained to the senior partner, who had been a junior one to my father, and all I got by it was being set to make a copy of a marriage settlement some fifty years old, and no more wanted for any purpose than a visit from the Pope. Upon this I put on my hat, and calling on an eminent solicitor in the City, told him the state of affairs. He said, "Oh, that will never do. I am sorry I can't take you into my office, as I have no vacancy for an articled clerk; but I will give you a letter of introduction to some friends who I know want a gentleman like yourself to assist them in conveyancing and chancery practice."

This was the very thing for me, as these were the branches to which I had been giving my attention. I immediately went off to deliver my letter of introduction, and had a long interview with the senior partner. He told me that he wanted an abstract made of a deed, and asked if I would stop and do it for him. I set to work in his office, and soon finished it. It was then arranged that I should go back, and announce my intention of leaving, and he would write that evening to the firm, stating that he had seen me, and was desirous of taking an assignment of my articles, at his own expense, as soon as possible.

When I got back, the senior partner of the firm had gone home; so that the first intimation which he got of my intention to quit the old shop was Mr. Clarke's letter. In the morning, as I expected, I was soon summoned into the "great presence," when I was asked in a somewhat peremptory manner, "What was the meaning of the letter" that had been received. "Did I want to leave? If so, he should be glad to know why." To which I simple replied, "I did wish to leave, and had made up my mind to do so; the reason being that there was nothing to be learnt in his 'gentleman's office.'" I was then asked, "Is your father aware of this step?" "No," I replied, "but he is aware that I am dissatisfied. I have consulted some of his old friends in the profession, and am acting under their advice." The senior partner then said curtly, "Very well, I shall write and say that this being the case, I will execute the assignment as soon as it is ready." I replied, "Then, with your permission, I will take my seat in the new office to-morrow morning." He looked somewhat astonished, and said, "Oh, certainly; go when you like."

I then went into "the gentleman's office," and announced my departure, which caused a little commotion; and it appeared one of the gentlemen had already complained of having no means afforded him of gaining information; while another had written home with the request that he might be taken away for the same reason. Then we all three adjourned for a walk on the Customs House Quay, to "blow the steam" off; and so ended all my prospects in the old concern, for which I had given up the one great desire of my life. After lunch, we devoted the afternoon to parading Regent-street; in the evening I collected all my goods and chattels at the old office, and the next morning, at ten o'clock, presented myself to Mr. Clarke. He was a little taken aback at my rapidity of action, but I was at once assigned a seat, and went "into harness," and this time I believe I stuck to the collar pretty well.

I here soon made the acquaintance of my principal's younger brother (as it turned out I was occupying the place vacated by him; he not having been able to get on well with the junior partner in the concern). He was a wonderfully nice and clever fellow, a thorough sportsman, too; and we used, whenever possible, to spend our holidays in shooting or fishing together; this soon ripened into a firm friendship, which ended only with his life, having lasted for nearly sixty years. Mr. Edward Salmon Clarke (or as he was always familiarly known as "Ted Clarke") was indeed a thoroughly good fellow in every sense of the word, and I still mourn his loss. Like me he hated the law, and did not remain long in it, after rejoining his brother. An uncle having left him a handsome fortune, he retired into Devonshire and kept and hunted his own foxhounds for a number of years on the borders of Exmoor; and it was only a short time before his death that he would give up the horn to a huntsman.

Of course I was down at my father's for the first of September, and we had some capital sport. We had a favourite spot for luncheon in the wood, a hundred yards or so above where the poacher got his involuntary cold bath, as before described. The stream here widened out into a broad space, which was one mass of the finest watercresses; near the right bank, in the middle of this bed, was a large round-topped stone standing about 6in. above the water. By rolling up the pockets of your shooting jacket, a seat might, with some little difficulty, be got on this – the right heel resting on the bank, and the left on another stone, placed, as if on purpose, out in the stream; here anyone could sit at ease, take his lunch, and pick watercresses, as required, to eat with it. Moreover, the drinking cup could be filled with the loveliest of pure water, which was so cold as to require qualifying with something from the flask.

My father never could be induced to essay perching on this stone, but my brother and myself used to take it by turns. One very hot day, when the stone was by right mine, my brother took it into his head, without saying a word, to bolt off and take possession. I, of course, remonstrated mildly, but he would not budge, and kept "crowing over" me by occasionally offering me a watercress, as those who were not on the stone had to get them from the bank as best they could, and then set down again to eat them. As my brother was reaching a long way to the left to get some extra fine cresses, the stone rolled from under him, and souse he went into some six or eight inches of water, and, as he went down on his elbow, he got a pretty ducking.

I very soon tipped the contents of my brandy flask down his throat, but, of course, there was no going home (some three miles) to get dry clothes, for it was on one of the early days in September, and there were heaps of birds before us, so he pulled off his things, which we wrung out, and hung up to dry in the sun, while, amid convulsions of laughter, he had to dance a jig on the bank to get warm in a singularly scanty amount of drapery.

In about an hour his things were fairly dry, and he rigged up, when we started again, and no harm came of it; but he said, "What the deuce could that infernal stone want by rolling over with me." I simply said, "Serves you right, old boy; if you had not taken unlawful possession, possibly I might have got the ducking, instead of you." He then remarked, "Confound it, there will no longer be a comfortable seat for having one's lunch on." I said, "No, I should think you would be disposed to sell your rights in it now." "Ah!" he replied, "wouldn't I, if I could get anyone to be fool enough to buy it." "Well," said I, "I'll give you sixpence for your right?" "Shell out, old fellow; it's yours for ever," was the answer, and so the transaction was concluded.

It had occurred to me that the stone could be replaced, perhaps more securely than ever, with a little trouble; so when my brother had to return to his drawing-boards, scales, and compasses, I proposed to old Sam that we should go up the first opportunity and see what could be done. We carried some bricks and sacks over one shoulder and our guns over the other and proceeded to the spot, took off our jackets, and turned our shirt sleeves up to the shoulder. We soon found that by building two piers we could replace the stone firmly. Then came the tug of war; it was a deuce of a lift to get the big stone up and place it on the piers, but we did it at last. The intense cold of the water caused sundry applications to the whisky flask, as we got pretty wet during the operation.

My brother shortly returned again, and we soon took that beat. I proposed lunching at the old spot, as usual, when he remarked, "What's the use of that, now the old stone is gone?" "Well," said I, "there are the watercresses at any rate." "Very well, then; I don't care." His astonishment was great when we arrived at the spot, and saw the old stone back in its place, but some inches higher out of the water. "Well," he said, "this is capital; we shall be able to enjoy the old place as before." "I shall," said I, drily. "What, you? Remember I'm your elder brother." "Quite true," I replied; "but remember you sold your rights to me and you received the money, which took the matter out of the Statute of Frauds. Perhaps, if you behave yourself, I may sometimes allow you to occupy the seat." "You be hanged," was the reply. However, in spite of the bargain, we still enjoyed the stone by turns.

May 28th 1898

SPORTING REMINISCENCES AND ANECDOTES X
BY "20,000 SHOTS"

SANCHO, HIS CLEVER WAYS AND WONDERFUL NOSE – SAM WOOD'S NARROW ESCAPE

OLD SAM AND I were at the gate one day, when a higgler came up with his cart, and running by its side was a little squatty, pot-bellied pup, very prettily marked, and, as I thought, fairly well bred. (This dog eventually saved old Sam's life.) As they came slowly up the hill I said, "My eye, Sam, what a pretty puppy; I wonder whether we could get him."

The man, seeing us, stopped to try and sell some of his wares; but we wanted nothing in his line, though we intimated we would not mind buying his pup if he would part with it. All this time I had been talking to the pup, and "chirruping" to him; he tucked his pretty head on one side, wrinkled up his brow, and looked the picture of intelligence. I picked him up and examined him; and the man said, "Oh, darn him, I wouldn't mind selling him; I can't get him along, and have to get out and put him into the cart constantly. What will you give for him?" We bid half a crown, and the man said, "Oh, master, a dry half-crown be blowed; give us a pint with it, and you shall have him." I replied, "You go up to the house with the gamekeeper, and you shall have two if you like; I will mind your pony while you are gone."

Thus we became possessed of the finest and most intelligent dog that I ever saw in my life. He was named "Sancho," and put at once into training, as he was about five or six months old. He looked a thoroughbred setter, was large and powerfully built, and black and white in colour – the black portions flecked with white, and the white spotted with black – splendidly feathered, and the most docile, good tempered, and teachable of dogs, with a wonderful nose. He had one curious defect, however, which caused us to think he had some cross of the Newfoundland dog in him; for occasionally, when very intent on his point, and close to his game, instead of carrying his stern straight out, setter fashion, he would turn the tip up into a curl, keeping it nervously twitched up and down with the regularity of a metronome; this often caused such mirth among our friends shooting with us, that they could hardly walk up to the point.

Nothing could equal Sancho as a retriever, and we often worked him simply as such, keeping at heel until wanted; and during the years we had him, it was known from the game-books that upwards of fifteen hundred head of winged game had been killed to this dog, without a single one that was seen to fall having been lost. One day he had a signal triumph: I was shooting with a gentleman who had four very active, quick spaniels; he shot a hen pheasant, which I saw fall in a roadway in the wood, instantly get on legs, and run into the "stuff;" Sancho was at my heel as retriever. My friend put his spaniels on the bird, but they could not recover it. After about a quarter of an hour's fruitless hunt I suggested that he should go on shooting at the other end of the wood, and I would try Sancho for the last bird.

When my friend had got out of hearing I took Sancho up to the spot, put to his nose a feather which was still lying where the bird fell, and told him to "go seek." He ran a few yards along the road, and then entered the "stuff," which was only two years' growth, so that I could see pretty well what was going on. He made a circuit, and came out into the road a dozen yards above me, so that he had made a half circle, and came up to me and seemed to tell me that he could not hit off the scent; and no wonder, since these four wild spaniels had travelled over every yard of the ground. I told him, however, to go in and try again, while I myself never left the spot where the bird fell. This time Sancho was gone a good quarter of an hour, and I began to think he must be "standing" the bird somewhere, so I called and whistled him, well knowing that he would leave his point, return to me, and then lead me to the spot. But he did not answer my call, and several more minutes elapsed, when, happening to cast my eyes into the field next the covert, I saw him emerge from the wood on the opposite side with the bird in his mouth, and he galloped as hard as he could across the field, straight back to where he had left me. In a few seconds more he was at my side, with the winged pheasant in his mouth perfectly alive. He must have followed that bird over a quarter of a mile; and I call this a triumph of clever retrieving. He was thoroughly blown, but looked as "pleased as Punch" when he put the bird into my hand.

This dog had a wonderful memory, and I have sometimes in the winter, when alone, shot four or five pheasants during my beat and not caring to carry them about with me all day, have scratched holes in the dead leaves, placed birds in the holes, covering them up, telling the dog to "mark the spot." On returning home in the dark, on approaching these places I would say, "Sancho, go for the birds," and trudge on towards home. Sometimes he might have to go over a quarter of a mile to some of these hoards, but he never once failed to bring me the birds.

One day, I went out by myself with Sancho into one of the "Squire's" woods, my own shooting, for an hour's sport. I walked straight to the coal pit, in the middle of the wood, as the most likely place to get at once on a cock pheasant; all hens being now spared, I hunted it round, and the dog soon came to a point. On walking in before him, to my astonishment (as it was quite early in November), I flushed a woodcock, and very soon knocked him over. These birds (if there is any life left in them) have a nasty trick of crawling in under any herbage there may be, and they are often difficult to find; so I sent the dog in at once, not liking to risk losing the first cock of the season. I never used a bell, going out in this way; as the old cock pheasants on hearing it, would invariably run as hard as they could go across that covert, down some hedgerow, and into the next, before they would think of stopping. Not liking to make a noise (as nothing scares game like the human voice), I walked on to look for the dog, and found him three or four yards to the left of where the woodcock fell. There stood the dog – as stiff as a crutch excepting the tip of his tail – pointing into some bracken, with the woodcock in his mouth, quite alive; its head was curling up behind the old dog's nose. Thinking there must be a rabbit there, I went a little round to where I could better see to shoot when the animal bolted, but nothing moved. I closed up until I was within two or three yards of the dog's nose, and from under my very feet up rose a splendid old cock pheasant, nearly as long as my gun, and went "cuckupping" as he went. When he had gone a proper distance, he was knocked over; then the old dog ran up to me, pushed the woodcock against my hands, and started off for the pheasant without being ordered (as doubtless he was it might be a runner), and was back with the bird quite alive long before I had finished loading, quick as I was over that process. I have often speculated whether Sancho could have seen that pheasant; but I think not, as the bird rose 9ft. or 10ft. from him, and the bracken was thick and partly broken down, and quite brown from the frost. If not, what a wonderful power of nose must that dog have possessed to detect, and point one kind of game while he had another alive in his mouth!

On another occasion I wanted to get some outlying pheasants that were in a dangerous place; I had nearly three miles to walk

SANCHO CARRYING THE FLASK

to the spinney; when I went in, Sancho soon found me a bird, which I shot. On proceeding to reload I found I had come away without my powder flask; there was a pretty go, but I tore a strip off my lunch paper, and wrote upon it, "Send my powder flask by the dog," then I told him to go home and bring me what they gave him. Having first put the slip of paper into his mouth, I sat down on the gate to await his return. He was wonderfully quick in getting over the six miles, but he brought me my flask all right. I shot a couple of brace of pheasants and a partridge, for six more shots, and then returned home.

It was the common custom at the house to send this dog down to the "shop" – one of those universal emporiums, where anything could be bought, from a lady's dress to a rasher of bacon. A note of what was required would be written on a slip of paper and put in a basket; he was then told to "Go to Chapman's," and off he would go. Anything ordered – eatables or not, even eggs – would be brought safely, and he would be

SANCHO GOES SHOPPING

back with his load before a man could have walked there. It was a good half mile.

We used frequently to take Sancho out of a night with us, and perhaps in the dark might not see him for a considerable time; but if anyone approached, he would be at our heels, muttering a low growl, as much as to say, "Here's somebody – look out;" and I feel certain that had anyone interfered with either of us, he would have gone straight at the man's throat. The way he saved Sam's life was through his intelligence in instantly understanding and obeying what was said to him.

Sam Wood had one night gone out by himself (though I was sleeping at the lodge), as he thought I should be too tired to go, having been shooting all day; and therefore he said nothing to me about it. Between twelve and one, a terrific thunderstorm came up suddenly, and he made for a hut that we had in one of the woods, and which we had bought from the charcoal burners after the last "cut." It was something like a gipsy's tent, formed from the sticks left for coaling, and was not more than about 6ft. in diameter. When we bought it, we dug a deep trench round the outside, with a drain out to the low ground, so as to keep it thoroughly dry. Inside we dug out a circle, not so deep by some inches as the outside drain, so that the natural ground formed a seat all round. We also added a door with posts and lintel, and a latch and padlock outside. It was perfectly wind and water tight, as we covered it with thick turves.

The rain came down terrifically, and old Sam, with his gun in a bag, and Sancho, just got in in time. When the storm was clearing off he was in a half drowsy state; the place was very comfortable inside, being half-filled with dry brakes; moreover, we always kept a gin bottle and glass there, besides powder and shot. There was a hole in the door, through which the finger could be put to raise the outside latch. This suddenly became obscured, and in an instant Sam knew some one must be there; and as the padlock and key were hanging outside, he at once made for the door, which one had to stoop to get out of. He then found himself face to face with the greatest scoundrel within ten miles round. The dog sought to follow him, and partly opened the door, when Wood called out "You stay there till I call you." There he stood opposite this ruffian, who had his gun pointed at Wood's chest. Sam cocked his gun inside the bag as he held it at his hip, and he told me he knew he fumbled at the trigger, and only wondered that he did not in his flurry fire the gun. So they stood for some seconds, when Sam said "Butcher, what do you do here at this time of night with a gun in your hand?" This was a mistake, as it showed the scoundrel he was known. Fortunately at this time, hearing his master's voice, the dog again moved in the hut, and was again told "to wait till he was called." But for this, there is little doubt, poor old Sam would have been shot dead. Butcher, thinking there was someone in the hut who would be a witness to the deed, stayed his hand. Had he fired, this noble dog would doubtless have broken out, flown at his throat, and never have left him alive. As it was, the man got uncomfortable, and began to edge off. Old Sam had the presence of mind and pluck to feign following him up, till the scoundrel broke into a run, when Sam started after him, shouting as loud as he could "Run up to the gate at the top, and trip him up as he comes over." The ruffian, probably thinking I should meet him at the top, and knowing pretty well that I should "stand on no repairs," redoubled his speed.

As soon as the fellow was clear off out of hearing, Wood returned to the hut, let Sancho out, locked the door, and made tracks for home. Even when he told me of the event next morning he was in a state of considerable excitement, saying it was "the narrowest escape" he had ever had, and that but for dear old Sancho he would have been murdered.

Although Sam was brave as a lion, his nerves were considerably shaken by the occurrence, and I told him he should never again go out at night alone when I was down there. However, Mr. Dick Butcher soon got into trouble; he was "wanted" for a little affair of sheep-stealing somewhere near Copthorne, and was "grabbed" near Croydon; and for this offence he got transported. He richly deserved to be hung for his "good deeds." However, we were very glad to be clear of him, as he was certainly the most reckless ruffian of all the poacher gangs of the neighbourhood.

September 10th 1898

SPORTING REMINISCENCES AND ANECDOTES XI
BY "20,000 SHOTS"

WORK AT NEW OFFICE – AMATEUR GUNMAKING AND EXPERIMENTS

AFTER MY MIGRATION to the new office I had no reason to complain of having nothing to do; for after a short time I found that I had not only all the practical part of the firm's equity business on my shoulders, but also a portion of the conveyancing, as I had to go into the titles, and prepare the abstracts, of all the property to be sold. As a necessary consequence my opportunities of getting a turn with the beloved gun or fly rod became fewer and farther between; but as time grew on I had a small bench placed in the corner of my room, on which I had set up a lathe belonging to my brother (he was now fully occupied in railway engineering).

By way of solace at getting so little time for the use of the gun, I made up my mind to try if I could not make one; so I invested in a pretty strong iron vice, set up a rest on the bench to support the gunmaking, got a pair of barrels of 22 gauge and 24in. long, and other necessaries; set to work in earnest. It was slow work at first, as I had not only to feel my way, but also to make a number of tools for myself – gunmaker's tools, such as dog-leg chisels, cutters (male and female), finders, &c., are seldom to be bought anywhere.

I had, of course, to stick to my work at the office, so I divided my time pretty much as follows: Up about six; a couple of hours' work at the bench and gun; dress and breakfast by nine; get to the office by ten and work till almost half-past five; dine at six; then about two hours at reading law books; then another spell at the gunmaker's bench; and get to bed about eleven. Of course, on any nights that I went to the opera or musical parties this programme had to be altered; but I always made it a rule to read up on Sunday evenings any hours I had so missed during the week.

On my first coming to London I had great difficulty in finding out how and where I could carry out any gun experiments I wished to try; but, as before stated, I found that there was a shooting ground with an excellent plate at a place called Copenhagen House in the Islington Fields, about two and a half miles off. (At this time I lived in the neighbourhood of Russell-square.)

Just at this time a lady made me a present of a beautiful double barrel 16-bore by Rigby, of Dublin. She told me in her letter that she had sent all the way to Dublin for it because her father, who was an Irishman, always declared that there were no guns equal to Rigby's. It was indeed a handsome present, and I highly valued it; and though this was over sixty years ago, I still have some of the impedimenta.

Four o'clock next morning saw me with this gun under my arm, on my way to Copenhagen House. The gun suited me to the life – the barrels being only 27in., and light and handy. It shot exceedingly well, and was for a long time a favourite. I must confess, however, that eventually, when my home-made little gun got into a state that it could be shot in the "soft," I preferred that to the lightly, as it was 3in. shorter, and nearly 1¼lb. lighter.

I now began to try all sorts of experiments on the form of the inside of the breech, working first one and then the other, until I worked them out, then getting another pair in and trying further experiments. This took me several months, but as muzzle-loaders are now as thoroughly exploded as a fired cartridge, I will not waste time or space over this long series of trials. Suffice it to say that I found a considerable ellipse at the breech shot much better than the half-round base left by the ordinary cherry tool. Singularly enough, however, if this were carried to an extreme, and the bottom of the breech were left quite flat, the shooting was the poorest; and the farther towards the front of the charge I got the ignition, the better and the harder was the shooting. For this purpose I made nipples with a long projection beyond the thread, and screwed them into the breeches at the most obtuse angle to the bore of the barrels. I have some of these long-tube nipples still by me.

My boring bits were made so as to run in the lathe, or be worked in a brace. Of course, when this was done, the barrels had to be secured near the centre, but in such a manner that they could swing with every deflection in working the brace. However, in the long run, having satisfied myself, after endless trials, as to the best form of breech, I got my little gun to shoot quite as close and hard as any that I tried made by different gunmakers; in fact, they shot better than most, though some of my friends considered that they made rather too narrow a pattern. But, as, until choke-boring came up, I could never get a gun to shoot close enough to please me, I was well satisfied. Indeed, I always used to say that, if I could get a gun to throw every pellet in the charge into an 18in. circle at 40 yards, that would be the gun I should always prefer to shoot with; but I never could get it.

Altogether, I was so pleased with my first effort at gunmaking, that I had hardly finished this gun before I began another; it was of the same length, with a little larger bore – a 20. This time I sent to Clive, of Birmingham, for the best pair of stub-twist barrels that he could supply, as I no longer feared spoiling them. Afterwards I turned out three more double, of 14 and 18-bores, and another 22, and a rifle, all of which turned out well. The 14-bore only weighed 5¾lb. I shot with it for over twenty years, and then a gunmaker allowed me, in exchange, actually more than the gun originally cost me. It was, I think, the handiest gun I ever had. This I attribute to a great extent to my having stocked it quite straight, *i.e.,* without any "cast off" whatever. At all events, I could never do better, except in very long shots, after choking came in. The gun I "chopped" for I did not like it, and sold it at the end of a week's shooting in Norfolk.

Of course, I dodged up and down to my father's as often as possible; but it was seldom, except during the long vacation, that I could get away longer than from Saturday afternoon to Monday morning, though occasionally I did get a day.

September 24th 1898

SPORTING REMINISCENCES AND ANECDOTES XII
BY "20,000 SHOTS"

ONE NIGHT IN the middle of August I had left the drawing-room about eleven o'clock to go over to the lodge (where I still always slept), and going out the back way I found old Sam in the lathe-room, where the loaded guns were always kept. If he knew I was coming, my own old single was always carefully loaded by him, awaiting my arrival. We had only been talking a few seconds, when I heard a distant "wow." I immediately said, "That's Joe Morris's brother." Another slight "wow" confirmed this. In an instant (though I was in evening dress) I snatched my gun from the rack, Sam seized his, which was leaning against the bench, the candle was put out, the shop locked up, and we started up the garden.

As we both felt certain that the sound came from a part of the "Squire's" ground known as the Beechen Shaw, about three fields off, we kept the dark side of the hedgerows, so as not to show ourselves in the moonlight. When we got near the place, he proposed we should divide, he going along one field to the left, and I the next field to the right, so as to get them between us. I passed along the side of the Beechen Shaw (a spinney some 150 yards long and bout 20 yards broad) until I came to the cartway that led to the bars into the next field. When within three or four yards of this, a hare came under the bars and almost crashed my legs as I stood in the shade at the side of the track. In another instant the dog leapt the bars, and landed almost at my feet. He at once "found of me," but before he could turn I threw up my gun and shot the dog in the chest; then I seized him by the tail and swung him into the covert. He was so heavy, however, that he fell hardly a yard from the track. I then popped in on the other side of the roadway and hid myself behind one of the trees from which the place took its name. I had hardly got out of sight, and quiet, before two fellows rushed down the track and stopped near to me. I placed my hands and face close to the tree (as the bare skin shows very white in moonlight) and kept my ears open, but my eyes shut – as if they get a glint of light upon them they shine like two sparks, and are certain to betray you. One of the fellows said, in an undertone, "the shot sounded somewhere here;" the other said, "Yes, it is that --- fellow Wood; if I could catch him, I'd break every bone in his body." Pleasant for me, with only an empty gun in my hand. I made up my mind, however, that if they discovered me I would jump out upon them, club the gun, knock down the nearest fellow, and make for the other.

At this moment a third man vaulted over the bars, and said, "Get away, you fools. Do you want to be caught? He would never have shot the dog if he had been alone. Now, bolt and separate." And to my great relief off they went.

Shortly afterwards another figure got cautiously over the bars; the moon was now partially obscured, so that, peeping with only one eye, I could not make out who it was; then came a low whistle (our well-known signal), which I answered, and stepped out of my hiding place.

"Come away, sir," said Sam; "they may come back." And we returned, still keeping on the dark side of the hedges. When clear away, he asked what I had done with the dog, as he had heard from the "yow" that the shot was fatal.

When we returned to the house, we found the doors of the court (where the workshop was) bolted. Everybody had gone to bed. We made our way silently through the stable yard, down the carriage drive, and over to the lodge. On getting in, Sam called to his wife to let her know who it was, and then said, "Now, sir, we must have no light, as we may be watched, but about two o'clock I'll get a sack (I know where to find one in the dark), and we'll go up and bring him home." I replied, "Certainly; you don't go by yourself, though; I shall go with you."

We sat down by the embers of the wood fire, and before starting he managed to load my gun again in the dark, and we crept out of the other door of the lodge, went through its verandah and down the plantation, so that nobody watching at the back of the lodge could see us depart. Watching in front was out of the question, on account of the road and the open space.

Sam told me that he was quite near enough to see the light of the flash of my gun when I shot the dog; and that, when Jack White jumped over the bars, he passed so close to him (as he lay hidden in the ditch) that he could have touched him, or tripped him up. "But that was not my game," he added; "if they had discovered you I should have been over in an instant; and when they found there were two of us they would have been sure to bolt, as they never like two together (one to support the other); though where there was only one they would sometimes brave it out."

This exactly confirmed what old Bell had often told me, that "they would stand and fight with one man," but if there were two, so that one could support the evidence of the other, "they would not risk the certainty of conviction" if brought before a magistrate.

When we neared the spot, Sam asked if I knew where I had thrown the dog. I said "Yes, to an inch; he is just in there" (pointing to the spot). Sam said that he would go in at the bars, so as not to leave a track behind him. When he had advanced a little way, I said, "He is just before you, Sam, not a yard in." Directly afterwards I heard, "All right, here he is;" and in a few seconds he came out again with his sack load.

All this time it was quite dark, the moon being obscured by clouds; and we got back to the lodge without incident. Then Sam said, "Now, Master Arthur, we'll go to bed till about four o'clock, when we can bury him in the garden, and be in again before anybody is about. But recollect, no light, sir."

I groped my way up to my room, threw off my evening coat and boots, lay down on the bed, and was soon sound asleep. With the first glimmer of daylight I heard a footstep on the stairs (it was old Sam). "Now, Master Arthur," said he, "we'll go and bury the dog out of sight."

I jumped up and went down with him. I took the spade and he the sack, and we went into the garden (which skirted the high road). Sam had evidently made up his mind where the burial was to be carried out, as he walked straight to the root of a fruit-tree, and commenced moving the cabbages that were planted behind it. In a few minutes a hole some 2ft. deep was ready, and we turned him out of the sack. "Ah," he said, "that is Joe Simmon's lurcher sure enough." On examining him it was found that the nose and end of the lower jaw were blown away; the charge had then entered the chest, and gone out again just at the end of the sternum.

"How straight you must have shot," said Sam; "he must have been close to you."

"Yes," I replied, "not more than four or five feet from the muzzle of the gun."

The dog was then pitched into the hole, some earth thrown over him and trodden down; and this was repeated until the hole was filled up, then the cabbages were replanted, and the extra mould distributed between the rows.

At this time it began to rain. As we returned to the lodge Sam said, "This is good. If this rain goes on for a bit, not even the gardener will know that the ground has been disturbed."

We now stole in, and went quietly to bed. In the morning my old ally, Jemmy Gent, came, as usual, for orders. I happened to be in the workshop. Coming up to me, and looking at me pretty hard, he said, "You look as if you'd been up all night, sir. Were you out?"

"No, Jemmy." I replied. "You told us the gang were going over to Ford, so we did not trouble ourselves." He took his orders and went off.

Two or three days afterwards I met him in the road, and he gave me a sign to go down to the lodge. When we got down there he said, "My eye, sir, there is a deuce of a row."

"Why, what's up?" I asked.

He said, "Joe Simmons is furious at the loss of his dog, and says the gang had him that night. This they deny, but one of them told me 'we had him over at Ford right enough; but we were disturbed there, and crossed the hollow lane and went on to the Squire's ground. We were nearly caught there, and Wood shot the dog there is no doubt, though we did not see him.'"

"No," replied Jimmy; "I know that both Wood and Master Arthur were in bed that night."

"Well," said the poacher, "these beggars from Ford must have followed us across."

And so we escaped all blame of that business. Joe Simmons was a small farmer some four or five miles off; but the finishing of his dog was a really good riddance for the entire neighbourhood.

October 8th 1898

SPORTING REMINISCENCES AND ANECDOTES XIII
BY "20,000 SHOTS"

"NOT CAUGHT YET" – SNARING VERMIN – TRAPPING, AND BEST MODE OF SETTING TRAP

I WAS NOW GETTING more invitations for shooting than I could possibly find time to accept, as a kindly friend in London had introduced me to many county families, and if I could have left town for the grouse shooting there were several moors open to me. But that could not be; it was as much as I could do to get away for the 1st of September.

One day I was walking with the keeper over to one of the places I had been invited to shoot at, when we passed a shop in which was exhibited a print of a fox (with his head turned tremendously round) looking down from a bank upon a trap baited with a baby rabbit. It was splendidly drawn; and the fox was pretty fair, having much of the sly, sneaking expression they always have. I called the keeper's attention to it, and asked him what he thought of it. He looked at it for a moment, then read the title, "Not Caught Yet," and after a short pause added, "No, I should think not; as though any fox would be such a fool as to run into a trap set like that."

The comment was splendid; and it reminds me of the fact that I have never yet met with a gamekeeper who really knew how to properly set a trap; they, one and all (including old Sam Wood, who gave me my first lessons in trapping when quite a boy) set their traps on the ground. This very soon appeared to me to be an unmitigated mistake, as to get into the trap every creature not larger than a stoat or polecat had to go up a considerable step (an inch and a half or so) before it could get on to the treadle. This alone is quite enough to put a wily animal on the lookout, and in many cases will prevent his going in.

I soon saw a remedy for this. So, before I was sixteen, on going trapping, I always armed myself with a freshly sharpened table-knife, a gardener's trowel, and an old horse comb, in case I pitched in a grassy place. On arriving at the intended spot, the first thing to be done is to determine in which direction your expected victim would be most likely to come, then take care that the tail of the trap shall be in a different direction. Having first pressed down the spring, and confined it with the shackle, place the trap on the ground where you intend to set it; then cut closely round the outside with the table-knife, a couple of inches deep. If it is a grassy spot, before doing this the grass should be carefully combed straight away from the trap. Having removed the trap, take out the turf first, and then sufficient earth to let the trap in, so that the jaws and treadle (and the tail of the trap also) shall be exactly level with the general surface of the ground. Care should be taken that the edges of the ground are left perfectly square and unbroken, so that the trap, when set and placed in the opening, shall exactly fit it; then dig a round hole at the end of the tail, in which to drop the chain attached to the trap, and the ring may be pegged at the bottom, if thought necessary. Set it as lightly as possible, slide back the shackle, and place the trap gently in the opening; put the bait on the treadle, sprinkle a little mould on the other part, and place a few dead leaves about, but so that when the trap is sprung they will not be shut up in the jaws; comb the grass back over the trap as far as it will reach, and then as it is growing, it will slip off as the trap closes; drop the chain into the hole, lightly fill it in with mould, and the thing is done.

I am certain that two traps set in this manner will catch more vermin in a given time than a dozen set in the old-fashioned way. Some keepers always tie the bait on to the treadle, unless suspended over the trap. This is another great mistake, as, should the animal not spring the trap at once, his first impulse is to drag the bait away. In trying to do this he lifts it, when, being tied, treadle and all come up together. The effect of this is that the hinged lever, which goes over one jaw of the trap and then engages in a notch in the top of the treadle above its hinge, is driven down to its extreme end, instead of being left as when set, just at the edge, so that a slight weight will slip it out and spring the trap. This notch is fully an eighth of an inch deep, as generally made. No animal lighter than a cat will sufficiently depress the treadle of the trap to spring it; and long before this the vermin are generally clear off.

I have more than once known another grand mistake made by trappers. It has been said to me, pointing to the traps, "There they be, sir, all fresh 'iled' and ready to set." Now, this oiling process is often carried out with salad oil from the house (too rancid for use), or perhaps even horse oil. The smell from this alone would keep most things out of the trap for a fortnight at least; and there are some creatures you want to trap for occasionally which are so wary that even the scent of a man's hand on the trap will keep them out for days. The best plan is to thoroughly scald the traps intended to be used, and while they are drying and cooling get a little blacklead (there is always plenty in the house for cleaning grates) and rub this down with some fresh lard into a thick paste; put on a pair of gloves, pick up one of the traps, and with a piece of wood cut to a flat point put this blacklead paste into all the working joints. Move them backwards and forwards until they work quite easily, not forgetting the ends of the square mortice in the spring that works over the jaws, and also the edge of them where it rubs up in closing when sprung, and so on with the lot. Never handle a trap without gloves; if you do, some vermin will not go in for days. Some creatures can hardly be got into a trap under any circumstances; but such as these can generally be snared.

As I have commenced the subject of trapping, I had better now go on with my own experiences in the management of coverts and preservation of game. I feel some difficulty in describing my method of snaring, as I was once "let in" by a neighbouring gamekeeper. Sam Wood had told him of my success in this mode of snaring, and he came to me for further information, saying that he wanted to catch a troublesome dog. I innocently told him how to set the wires, and how, by means of a bender, the dog could be hung. (The actual *modus operandi* I think I had better keep to myself, for reasons which will be obvious presently.) I told him the chief thing was to ascertain where the animal came out into the open, and where he popped in again, telling him that "All creatures, before going out to show themselves, move very slowly, and cautiously peep out. If there is no cause for alarm, the whole head will come out, and the animal will look around; then, if the coast is quite clear, he will move out gently and trot off to where he goes in again, and almost always, when travelling that way, he will keep to the same track. Now, when he gets to the spot to go in, he is instinctively anxious to get out of sight as quickly as possible; so he jumps in with a bound. Just over where he alights inside is the spot to pitch the wire; his head goes into the noose, and he is caught before he finds it out."

I was away in London just afterwards, and did not see this man again for about a fortnight. On meeting him I naturally asked how he had got on. He replied, "Lor, sir, I ketched the dog the fust night, and the vixen the next; they was both hung and dead before I got to 'em next mornin." So it seemed I was the innocent cause of this piece of vulpecide.

At the time, however, I certainly believed that he was speaking of a hound of singular egg-sucking proclivities, who not only visited our coverts, but also our hen-roosts. This hound was caught in the same manner, but not hung; he was taken home to his master, whereupon the hanging process was carried out by him.

October 29th 1898

SPORTING REMINISCENCES AND ANECDOTES XIV
BY "20,000 SHOTS"

HABITS AND WAYS OF GAME – WINGED AND FOUR-FOOTED VERMIN, AND HOW TO DESTROY THEM

AS I HAVE BEEN LED INTO a little "keepering" business, I think I had better go on with it. Possibly there may be some sportsmen in these days of "driving" and "slaughter" who may still like to know something of the ways and habits of the game, not which they pursue, but which are driven to them to be killed, as also of the creatures, usually designated vermin, that are the natural enemies of all game, both feathered and four-footed.

Hawks give gamekeepers a lot of trouble; and if one is shot on the nest, the mate never returns to it but once, and usually finds out if anyone is watching for him. His one visit is generally made by dropping like a stone from a height into the nest; and no one can be quick enough to shoot him at this time. If the nest has been robbed, as well as shot through, he never returns to it even once, as he can see what has been done the first time he flies over.

Hawks are very fond of perching on the top of poles, particularly the division known as "the harriers," and will even sit on the posts of a common ox fence; but prefer a pole 8ft. or 10ft. high. These poles are frequently to be found on shootings, put up purposely by the keepers, and they soon get to be known and used; but the time occupied in laying up to get a shot at them is indeed an "unknown quantity" with a vengeance. A keeper may sometimes waste the best part of three or four days without getting a shot. Now, this will never do if he has much ground to look after, so I invented a plan for catching the hawks alive in wires. A fine brass wire was passed through the fire to thoroughly soften it and take off all the glare of the metal. A small round eye was turned in it round a bradawl. This wire was long enough to pass through a staple driven in the pole about 1ft. from the top, and to that end was attached a string, to which was appended a leaden plummet, an old horseshoe, or even a stone of sufficient weight. I noticed that the hawks on leaving a pole always dropped off it, somewhat in the manner of a bather when diving, and almost always in the same direction. A round noose about 3in. in diameter was set in the wire; a notch was cut in the top of the pole, into which the wire was lightly drawn; the noose was so arranged as to stand horizontally about 1in. above the top of the pole, projecting beyond it on the side the bird generally "took off"; the weight was then allowed to hang below against the pole. The hawk, on settling, put one or both feet through the noose; and, on diving off the pole, the bird pulled the wire out of the notch, when the falling weight instantly drew the noose tightly down on any part of the foot inclosed within it, and the bird was a prisoner until you came to take him out. But this was a matter of caution, and strong gloves must be used, as the birds have powerful beaks and claws, and know how to use them too. I have never known anyone, save the few keepers I have taught myself, pursue this excellent plan; and it has another advantage: the keepers can send the birds alive to the nearest naturalist dealer, and make a few shillings by them.

On one occasion I used a round pebble as a weight. This slipped out of the typing, and the bird, of course, dragged wire and string through the staple, and, for anything I know to the contrary, may still be about with the snare attached to him. Crows and magpies may (?) be caught in the same manner; but they are much more difficult to capture, being more erratic in their habits.

Rats are a class of vermin that a great many gamekeepers unaccountably keep out of their reckoning; and yet there is nothing much worse for the game preserver. It is not, I believe, very generally known that there are two partial migrations of these pests every year (perhaps it had better be called "change of quarters"). Sometime – in June usually – the great bulk of these pests leave the houses, homesteads, and stackyards, and go into the fields, remaining there until some little time after the harvest; then they return to the delights of the sewers and piggeries. But they always leave behind them a few very old and powerful buck rats. These are frequently and quaintly called "old bachelors," as they no longer care for the delights of social life, but remain out by themselves, usually in rabbit burrows, which they metamorphose into citadels of their own (after turning out the lawful proprietors), and they are veritable fiends in a game preserve. They are strong enough to surprise and kill full-grown rabbits, though hares frequently escape them; but when young leverets appear, and, still earlier, young rabbits, they are readily killed and greedily devoured.

Hen pheasants have a very silly habit of dropping eggs about promiscuously in all sorts of places, often ten or a dozen or more, before beginning the serious business of nesting. Really good keepers will look for and find a lot of these, and set them under hens; but any that are not found are certain to be hunted out and duly sucked by the rats; and thus (if they have not previously acquired it in the hen-roosts of the farms) it gives them a taste for egg-sucking, and they will hunt out, and eagerly devour at a meal, the entire contents of both pheasants' and partridges' nests. This is really the common cause of the small coveys of squeakers so often found at the commencement of the season, as the rats will sometimes destroy two or three nests of eggs in various stages of the same birds; but if they can catch the hen, she too is eaten. Occasionally these "squeakers" arise from the hen having hatched very early, and, the old cock having taken off the brood, the hen will lay again; but this is seldom the case as compared with the cause above referred to.

When the pheasants, and afterwards the partridges, hatch, the destruction is awful; nearly a whole nest of young poults will be sacrificed at a meal. These infernal "old bachelors" are difficult to exterminate; but it can be done. They can seldom be shot, as they prowl in the open very late, and are such a dark grey that they are difficult to see; and but few ferrets will tackle them in their holes. It is next to impossible to get the rats to go into a steel trap; they have been too well educated as to these during their residence in the farm outbuildings; but they may sometimes be caught in a trap deftly set on the level, as before described.

The best plan, however, is to wire them. The burrows or holes they frequent in the hedge-banks can be seen at once, as the nature of the soil turned out by rats is so widely different in appearance from that of rabbits. The snare should be set near the centre of the run, the bottom of the noose being about 1½in. from the ground, or a little more, and should have a strongish bender; this may be kept down by any of the various means of wedges and pegs, to be discharged when the snare is moved. Mr. Rat is usually caught round the neck and one foreleg; his effort to get that one back, or the other one through, spring the bender, when up he goes.

A heavy bit of paving stone or iron plate, set with the usual figure of 4 arrangement, will also succeed; but the ground it falls on must be very flat and level. A strong half-circular wire spring trap that nips him across the back, will also generally succeed. The best baits for these traps is a piece of good strong cheese well toasted, or a bit of red herring, kept till it has got a little "gamey."

I consider these pests so abominably destructive that I have often doubted whether it would not be better to spare the polecats of the neighbourhood as the lesser evil of the two. These bold marauders will always collar the biggest and strongest rats. But all gamekeepers should be told to give a special attention to the "old bachelors."

Jays and magpies are, I think, not nearly so mischievous as gamekeepers often consider them, though both will undoubtedly at times suck eggs and also pick up young chicks. Magpies are difficult to dispose of, except by the gun. Their nests are usually at the tops of very high trees, but they may generally be shot during the nesting time. Jays nest lower down, in the coverts, and can mostly be got during this time; but if they hatch you may be certain of them by securing the young "squabs" with a piece of soft brush-wire secured round one leg, the other end being fastened to a bough. The old birds are sure to come to feed their young, and can then be shot. Both these birds are very difficult to either trap or snare.

Crows require special attention, particularly the grey or hooded kind; and rooks are nearly as bad. They are perfect fiends at egg-sucking, and never miss a chance at either tender young bird or beast. They are difficult to get near, they are so very wary; but you can sometimes, as the Norfolk folks put it, "happen of them" and knock them over. They will seldom go into a trap; but there is one plan certain, so far as the grey crows go. These birds, when they find the nest of either pheasant, partridge, or grouse, visit it once a day, choosing generally the time the hen leaves for the "feed" in the afternoon. He shoves his hard beak into an egg, and then partially opens the mandibles. This gives him a double advantage; the egg will not slip off, and he can suck the egg as he flies away with it. He then goes straight to water (pond or stream), where he completes the sucking process until the inside of the egg is almost as clean as though wiped out with a sponge. Then he proceeds into the water an inch or two, carefully cleans his beak and the feathers round of all trace of the egg, and flies off, visits another nest, and brings another egg to the spot, to be similarly treated; so that the mischief worked by a few pairs of these birds on moor or manor is almost incalculable.

A keeper can always find these washing places readily enough by the egg-shells left; he should then build a pier out into the water until it is 16in. or 18in. deep, taking care that just the end of the pier is an inch or so under water; on this place a steel trap, so nicely balanced that on springing it will drop off the pier into deep water. One of the sucked eggs is then taken, placed on a pointed stick, and stuck into the bottom of the pool, so that the sound end is upwards, looking as though it were floating in the water, just within reach of the end of the pier. Mr. Crow will be certain to "twig it," and walk out to the end of the pier to secure it, step into the trap, and by its weight will be carried under water and drowned. In this manner a whole country may be cleared of these pests; but remember, if any mistake is made, so that the bird can squall or flutter long enough above water to attract the attention of his comrades, not another crow will ever walk out on that pier; it should be at once removed, and another erected at some other washing place.

These birds and other may be got by what is termed "funnelling." Get some paper nearly the colour of the soil of the field you intend to operate in, tie a strip of carrion with a bit of twine in the middle, hold this in the fingers, and turn up a funnel after the manner the grocers put up their sugar. Make it about large enough at the top to let in the bird's head, and 3in. or 4in. deep; twist up the bottom, then draw the twine through as far as the carrion will let it go, and secure round the twist with a clove hitch; cut off the long point at the top, and smear a little birdlime round inside. Place these about at intervals, nearly upright, in the fields which the crows frequent. They will very soon scent and find the carrion, and push their heads in to get it; the birdlime sticks to the feathers round the neck and head, and they can seldom get it off. The birds can then be approached at times near enough to be killed with a stick. If they attempt to fly, they mostly, from want of vision, keep going up and up, and present a very easy shot. Magpies, rooks, and jays may be also taken in this way.

Men sometimes bait these funnels with a little corn, or two or three beans, under the idea of getting some woodpigeons; but this is a mistake, as you may often "funnel" your pheasants and partridges and do a lot of mischief.

Hawks and falcons I have before spoken of, but I think the kestrel or windhover should be spared. The birds do not often offend by killing game, unless much driven by hunger; and I think they may be pardoned this for the sake of the good they do in carrying off the before-mentioned abominable old buck rats.

By-the-way, in speaking of them, I ought to have said that it is the grey Hanoverian rat which is so viciously mischievous to the game, I have never yet seen the indigenous English brown rat engaged in these depredations. Possibly, this may be from the fact that they are now so rare. The reason is that their loving brothers from Hanover have nearly exterminated and devoured them.

Owls, the white barn kind particularly, should never be interfered with, as they, too destroy the rats. Some keepers say that the brown short-eared owls are destructive to game; but I have never once caught one *in flagrante delicto*. I have, however, several times seen them shot early in October, in mistake for woodcock.

Stoats and weazels are easily disposed of with traps sunk to the level, and placed judiciously. Polecats are not quite so easy to catch, being much more wary. Martens, I fear, are now extinct in England. I have never seen one wild in my life.

House cats, when they take to poaching, are a terrible scourge, and give a gamekeeper no end of trouble, as they proceed on a plan of "one down and t'other come on"; for an old woman no sooner misses her cat than she gets another, which, from being imperfectly fed at home, soon takes to roaming the coverts. They are, I think, worse than a fox; for the reason that they travel a considerably smaller space of ground, while they kill as much. They are pretty easy to trap, however. Place a sunk trap against a bank, quickset hedge, or stiff sold bush (taking care that the tail of the trap is entirely clear of the way the cat must enter). Suspend the bait about 16in. or 18in. above the trap, cut two little thick and sturdy furze bushes, and stick these firmly in the ground, one on each side of the trap, so that pussy must go over it to smell at the bait; and then she drops here fore feet on to the treadle.

But, in spite of what I have said above, it is astonishing the distance cats will sometimes travel from their homing propensities. A farmer that we knew something of once moved nearly six miles across country, and his cat gave us infinite of trouble, as she would spend a few weeks at her new home, and then a few at the old one. Some of our best shooting lay right in her road, and she did us no end of mischief. She could never be induced to go into a trap, and it took us nearly three years (though she was frequently seen) before she could be shot. Every now and then she would treat us to a litter of kittens on her way, which were, of course, perfectly wild in all their habits, and were dreadfully mischievous.

We had another very bad cat that belonged to an old woman who lived in a cottage not more than 120 yards from our outside fence. It ravaged all that side of the "squire's" ground, as well as our plantations and hedgerows, which were full of rabbits, with a fair sprinkling of hares. This old brute, too, would never go into a trap, and, although she had several hairbreadth escapes, never got shot at but once. She was then pretty well peppered, which only made her the more wary, until one day Tom Knight, our dog boy, saw her walking along the top of one of our home fields; he ran and got the gardener's gun, stole up the hedgerow, concealed himself, and waited till puss came through the gate, when he instantly shot her. This was a really good riddance; but the fun of the story is to come. About a fortnight afterwards Sam and I were passing the old lady's cottage, where she and her little grand-daughter were out gardening, when she eagerly asked "if we had shot or seen her cat lately?" We could both conscientiously reply, like Macbeth, "Thou canst not say I did it." The old woman deplored her loss, saying "she was such a splendid mouser; there was not a rat or mouse about the cottage." Then the child took up the running and said, "Yes, granny, and you know there was never a day she did not bring home a hare or a rabbit." "Yah, you little fool," she said, and giving the child a sound box on the ear, bundled her howling into the cottage, shut the door, and said to me in a carneying (sic) voice, "You won't mind, sir, what a chi'd like that says."

Of course, we looked at each other, and burst into a loud roar of laughter.

November 5th 1898

SPORTING REMINISCENCES AND ANECDOTES XV
BY "20,000 SHOTS"

FOXES AND PHEASANTS

NOW I AM AFRAID I must touch upon a subject that I would rather have left alone – namely, foxes and pheasants. But before I began it I consulted some old friends on the point; and although they differed as widely as possible in their views as to foxes and pheasants being preserved in the same coverts, they all, in the main, agreed on one point, *i.e.,* that I should be expected by my readers to give my opinion on the matter, as I must have had at my age a considerable experience.

One old friend – a thorough foxhunter – took so broad a view of it that, having his permission, I shall, as nearly as possible, give his own words; the only condition put upon me being that I should not give his name, as he would rather some members of his hunt did not know what his opinions actually were.

He said, "Now, old fellow, look here; you've asked me a question or two, and I feel bound to answer them. You know I am a thorough foxhunter, though I occasionally take the gun (as I have done with you many a time), and I feel pretty certain most of your readers will expect, and like to have, your candid opinion as to shooters preserving foxes for the hounds. So speak out, and don't be like the old man and his ass – try to please everybody. Say what you think now on this point, and I feel certain that even those who don't agree with you will respect your straightforward honest views on this subject. From what you have been saying to me, I feel pretty certain, if both sides will take your hints as they are intended, it will lead to a better feeling. Now, you know, I am as inveterate a flyfisher as you are; but supposing you were a troller, do you think I would introduce pike into my trout river for your sport at the expense of my own? No, I am not such a fool. Yet this is just what many foxhunters expect; but I feel pretty sure your moderate views as just expressed to me will be acceptable to all."

After this admonition I think I had better fall into his views, and, dangerous as I know the ground is, at once walk boldly over it. I have always thought that shooters and foxhunters should work together on the give-and-take principle; but, as the Irishman put it, "the reciprocity should never be all on one side." I think it equally bad for a proprietor or shooting tenant to say the foxhounds shall never draw any of his coverts as for the M.F.H. to think he has a right to visit those coverts at his own sweet will. On all the ground I have ever had any control over I have always said, "Let there be a fox to be found whenever the foxhounds come," and I am quite certain that it is in the interest of game preservers that this should be so; *but the time and the covert to be drawn should always be arranged beforehand, to the convenience of both parties.* It is to the interest of the shooter for this reason, that the hounds are thrown into a wood or spinney where it is known there is a fox; and this suits the foxhunter, too, as Master Reynard is roused, got away at once, and a run is secured. Now, as the hounds in drawing a covert undoubtedly do most mischief in an hour than a fox would do in a month, it is far better that *one* covert should be thoroughly routed out than two or three disturbed. When foxhounds get into a thick wood, if they do not find a fox at once, you may rely upon it everything clothed in fur or feathers goes out. Huntsmen will always tell you that their hounds are perfectly free from riot, and will hunt nothing but their fox. No doubt this is so; but I believe I never saw the hound that would not "chop" every hare, rabbit, or pheasant that he gets a chance at. He does this involuntarily on the spur of the moment, but will leave it the instant it is killed, and will go on looking up his fox. This fact does not make it any better for the game preserve. And, further, huntsmen often throw their hounds into a covert without any consideration of whether they drive the game towards the middle of the shooting district or off on to a neighbour's ground, generally giving their hounds the wind, in which case, if they are on the lee side of a shooting (as pheasants mostly fly down wind), they go right off; and if that neighbour happens to be of the greedy, pot-hunting kind, which is too often the case, the unhappy shooting tenant may think himself lucky if 40 per cent. Or so of the hens which he had left for stocking the neighbourhood get safe back into his coverts; as there is no doubt that game driven out by foxhounds are so scared and demoralised that they settle and crawl into all sorts of outlandish places, and do not recover from this for several hours, falling easy victims to the first prowling cat, fox, stoat, or shepherd's dog coming that way. As many are killed in this way as by the neighbouring guns.

I have several times been told, and once by a gamekeeper, that foxes do no harm in a pheasant covert if there are plenty of rabbits; and scores of times it has been said that where rabbits are in plenty the foxes will not touch anything else. I wonder whether any one of these individuals would venture to tell you that a fox under these circumstances never robs a hen-roost. There can be little doubt that those who make such statements are people who can have had no experience of their own, or were woefully deficient in powers of observation. The truth is that foxes, like other carnivorous animals, are fond of a change of diet, and will never miss an opportunity of securing a tender young fowl or pheasant poult, more especially as these, particularly if hand reared, are as silly and stupid with regard to taking care of themselves as barndoor chicken. Is it to be expected that a fox will take the trouble of securing a rabbit instead when such delicate morsels are to be got for a quarter or less of the difficulty? If this were not so, why is it that we find in places where all are plentiful a number of chicken or pheasants killed and buried? There can be no doubt who does this!

One of the greatest difficulties a gamekeeper has to contend with (where foxes are preserved) is the keeping them out of the pheasant coverts. I have known many dodges tried, but fear there is no reliable remedy, as most of the things, if offensive, are likely to drive the pheasants out of the covert as well as keep the foxes from entering.

I have known gamekeepers to hang up traps about 6in. from the ground, on short stakes, under the idea that a fox knows a trap in any position; these are placed in gateways, rides, and tracks, and certainly will answer for a time, but require constantly shifting in place, as well as putting in different positions on the stake; but I believe anything else equally conspicuous will answer quite as well. Pieces of bright tin hung on a bent stake, where they can swing and turn round in the wind, so as to reflect the light or the moon's rays, are better; but they should be hung up at sunset, or soon after, and removed at daylight, early in the following morning, before the pheasants get on foot, otherwise they will be frightened quite as much as the foxes.

Another great point is to prevent the vixens having a litter of cubs in or near the pheasant covers; but this is by no means so difficult. A good keeper will be sure to know her haunts, and where she is likely to lay up. He should then borrow a syringe from the gardener, and procure some of the commonest and most offensive paraffin oil possible, place the rose of the syringe as far as he can into the earth, then squirt the paraffin as far down the earth as possible. The keeper should apply his nose to the earth, and, if he cannot smell the paraffin, repeat the operation. He must, of course, watch the vixen, to see if she selects another spot where she would be harmless. When she has kindled, he must daily shoot rabbits near round the earth; but must recollect it is no use to shoot them elsewhere, carry them and throw them down near. In this case the odds are twenty to one that the old fox will not touch them; and, though you may find them carried off, it has been by the farm labourers, who have appropriated them, or by hawks or crows. They should always be left untouched where they are shot. The scent of the human hand, hours and hours after, is too strong for the keen nose of a fox. If this is done regularly, but little damage will accrue to the pheasant preserve.

The great thing now is to keep the vixen away; and this will need all the diligence of the gamekeeper – aye, and his master too; for, if she once gets among the young pheasants, she will find them so easy to grab, and so tender and juicy for her cubs, that she will be perpetually there on the forage, and may be constantly seen, going back, with two to four in her mouth at a time.

Yet I have always said, "Let there be a fox for the hounds whenever they come." But this should always be by arrangement with the proprietor or game tenant, and then they should draw such places only as are pointed out to them as known to (in all probability) contain a fox.

Having said this much, I must turn to one grand redeeming point in "Master Charley's" character. He will never miss an opportunity of killing those abominable pests, the superannuated old buck rats, which I have before referred to. When foxes catch one of these, the first proceeding (in most cases) is to go for the brains. This they suck or lick out of the cranium almost as clean as if it had been done with a sponge; they then bury the corpse, to get a little high before eating it. They are very apt to leave the rat's tail above ground, so that the keeper readily sees what has been done, and can thank them for their assistance in that line.

I have written the above in order to show, as well as I am able to do it, what can be done to reconcile foxes and pheasants being on the ground at the same time; and my foxhunting friends will observe that I have not said one word as to their destruction by trap or otherwise. What I have said above has been penned under the conviction that if the views of shooters and foxhunters were better understood than they are, there would be between them much less ill-feeling and jealousy than I fear is now very often the case. I do hope and trust that what I have written may tend to this end; that foxhunters will be more considerate of the interest of the game preserver, in always drawing the coverts by arrangement; while the shooter will be more inclined to instruct his keepers to take care of the foxes where he can see his way to do so without endangering his master's sport.

November 19th 1898

SPORTING REMINISCENCES AND ANECDOTES XVI
BY "20,000 SHOTS"

THE IMPROVEMENT OF GAME COVERTS

WE CAN NOW TURN OUR ATTENTION to a much more agreeable section of the preserver's business, namely, what can be done in coverts to improve them and make them more agreeable to the game which they should contain.

In the first place, if there are any coverts with so decided and steep a slope towards the north that they get little or no sun at any time during the day, it is absolutely waste of time to try and get up a head of pheasants in such a locality. Feed or do what you will, they will not stop. You may occasionally find a cock bird or two to be shot, but the hens will scarcely ever resort or nest in such cold quarters; and it is better to devote such woods to rabbits. For this purpose, if the underwood is thin, it is a good plan to sow furze seed in open places, and to a considerable extent. Hares, also, do not like the cold side of a hill; but they may occasionally be found there – more frequently than pheasants. What all game prefer is a genial slope to the south. No pheasant covert can be perfect unless well supplied with good water; as pheasants drink a good deal, and it is not well for them to have to go too far for it. Sometimes these sloping coverts do not contain anything like a spring in the upper parts. They should always be carefully looked over to find any damp places. When found, a moderate hole should be dug, to see if water rises in it. If so, one of the drinking troughs, which I shall describe presently, should at once be placed there. Should the water be enough to overflow, it should be carefully conducted, by a shallow trench, as far as it will reach, when other drinking troughs can be put in suitable places. Should the lower part of the covert furnish a rill, however small, it should be utilised in the same manner, to its utmost capacity. The drinking troughs are made in this manner.

Get one or two common white dishes, about 20in. or 24in. the long way; turn them upside down on a board, and cover them with a softish paper; at each end place a piece of plastic clay on the paper on the rim of the dish, about half inch wide and quarter inch deep; spread it out against the slope of the dish. This, when the cast is made, will make an ingress and outlet for the water. Now cover the whole thing with Portland cement, and good, fine, clean sand, in the proportion of two of sand to one of cement; this will be thoroughly hard by the next day. A number of them may be made at a small cost of time and money. The dish, having the paper over it, will come out without the slightest difficulty, and will serve as a mould for as many as may be required. The dish itself must never be used, as very young chicks, when they go to drink, are very apt to slip in, and (the dish being glazed) get no hold for their little claws, and they never get out. Whereas, on the rough surface of the cement, they are out almost as soon as in. It is desirable to get a number of these troughs in every pheasant covert, and, when the water supply will admit of it, not much more than a hundred yards apart is desirable. The gamekeeper should keep two or three little heath or green broom brushes handy, so that every second day or so he can brush every impurity out of these troughs, which will immediately refill themselves with clean water. They should be sunk into the ground so that their edges all round should be quite on a level with it. Birds, both old and young, will constantly resort to them.

Where birds have to leave the covert for water, as is often the case, they are not only exposed to the public gaze of poachers, &c., but the young birds are very liable to be carried off by hawks, cats, stoats, or other prowlers. When the underwood of any such covert is cut, it is a very good plan to set out and trench segments of circles from 15ft. to 25ft. long, with the hollow side facing south. Plant these with laurel bushes 18in. high, and about the same distance apart; this gives the laurels a good start over the underwood. If the weather is very dry when planted, the station for each should have water poured into it before putting in the shrub. As soon as they are established stop all the lateral branches and about three out of every five of the leaders, choosing the tallest for stopping. This process should be gone through after every spring and midsummer shoots, as this induces them to grow thick as a wall. The large, shiny leaves of the laurel radiate a lot of heat from the sun's rays all through the winter, and here, on this account, all kinds of game will resort, being warmed by the sun, while the cold winds are kept off by the horns of the curve. The hollow from the chord of the arc need not be more than about 5ft. in 20ft. The number of these screens must, of course, depend on the size and formation of the covert, but they should not be too near any outside fence. If there is a woodcock anywhere about, he will be certain to be found in one of these retreats, especially if brakes grown thickly in front of it.

If any of these coverts are deficient in underwood, the proprietor (or game tenant), instead of cutting all the boughs away, should "plasher" as many as are required that can be thrown up hill. This process is carried out by chopping the bough about half through, 6in. or 8in. above the ground; on bending the bough down it will split for the 6in., and laterals that prevent it lying pretty flat should be chopped off. When the bough is on the ground, tongue some of the branches in convenient places, placing a small wedge across each tongue to keep it open; clear away the rotten leaf mould 5in. or 6in. deep, peg the bough firmly down into this with a strong hooked peg well driven in, cover up the place with the mould and tread it well in, thus in fact "layering" the "plashered" branches. These will soon root, and when they begin to grow the long ends should be stopped. Thus in even one season you get a much better covert for the game, while the growth of underwood is still more improved. These "layered" branches, where they take, always grow stronger and better than any young plants that can be put in, and sooner assume the coveted conditions of "stubs." Never throw the branches down hill, as the flow of sap through the half bough left alive is then checked, and the experiment does not succeed so well.

All feathered game wake up with the first streaks of light in the east, but they do not actually move for some time. Partridges that always "juck" in the open field give a cluck or two with the first glint of light; the hen and the young brood respond, the hen with a sort of purring noise, and the young birds with a smothered cheeping. This assures the old gentleman bird that all is right, and their heads soon go down again, but they sleep no more. With the first gleam of sunshine across the ground they commence to stretch themselves and run about to get their feathers dry, particularly if the night has been rainy, or the dew heavy. They run and gambol about in a most amusing way, presenting first one side to the sun and then the other. During this process they will drink any drops of dew that my hang on the herbage. As soon as they are all dry they will draw together again and remain quiet for about an hour or so. Then the old cock again gives the signal and they all fly off to the feed.

Pheasants being at this time in the coverts, are much more difficult to observe, and hares and rabbits are on foot pretty much all night, unless it should be extremely dark. But all kinds of game in the early morning like a place pretty dry under foot, where they can run about and dry themselves; and for this purpose pheasants, hares, and rabbits all leave the woods and disport themselves in the sunshine on the headlands on the east side of the coverts. Now, this is by no means desirable where it can be avoided, as it is an exposure to the public gaze of all passers-by, as well as to prowling vermin, and shows the poacher the principal part of the contents of every covert. This can be to a very great extent avoided by the proprietor (or the game tenant by his leave) cutting rides through the woods, pointing directly east and west. These need not be wider than 6ft. or 8ft., and, if made in four to six years of growth, need not be known to anyone but the master, his visitors, and the gamekeeper. They should never be carried nearer to any road or outside fence than 16ft. to 18ft., for the purpose of concealment. The underwood should be cut quite close to the stubs, which need not be in any way interfered with. The stuff cut should be tied into faggots and stowed away out of sight until a cart can be brought for them to carry them home. Should grass grow in the ride, or brakes, they should be kept cut down; as should also the young shoots of the stubs, that the game can run about in the sun in these tracks without encountering anything holding dew or raindrops, so as to wet instead of dry them in their morning's caperings.

All sorts of game will find these rides, and avail themselves of them and probably scarcely a tithe of what would otherwise be on the headlands go out at all to show themselves, until they move off later on to the feed. In a good large wood there should be several of these rides, so that the game has not too far to go through the wet underwood; moreover, these rides are exceedingly useful in the shooting season for the guns, for both winged and ground game.

I have many times seen open ditches, deep and narrow, cut straight across the coverts, under the idea of draining them; this is an abomination that should never be tolerated for a moment. They are quite unnecessary in a sloping wood, and in a flat one are worse than sepulchres for young pheasants, rabbits, and leverets. All fall in at times, but none ever come out alive; they have not the sense to follow the trench to its end, but waste their strength in trying to scramble out near where they have fallen in, until they fall back and die from exhaustion. If one of these fatal drains is searched in a well-stocked covert, a dozen to twenty infants, of all three kinds, may be found any day about the last week in May. In fact, I really believe the game preserver may calculate on losing in this way something like 50 per cent. of all the game bred in the wood; but the greatest number of victims are among the pheasants; four-footed game much more seldom fall in.

Hen pheasants are, of all things, about the most thoughtless, inconsiderate, and cruel of mothers; they will drag their young chicks after them through the wettest of coverts, then perhaps drag them over ploughed ground, until the poor little things get mired down, so that they are compelled to stop; but she goes striding on, calling repeatedly, but never heeding if her brood follow her. In this manner she may sometimes start with ten, and stop with only three or four; those left behind, as before said, mired down mostly die, as the mud dries round them, and the few who may survive are, of course, lost, and die later on, unless they happen to get picked up and joined to another brood. In the coverts, where the before-mentioned drains are dug, when she comes to one she opens her wings and hops over easy enough for her, but not so with the young chicks that cannot fly; but she calls and calls until they make the attempt. Most of them jump short, and fall in to die. Perhaps one or two may get safely across, and with these the hen goes on her way rejoicing. Those left behind soon perish of hunger and neglect, or fall an easy prey to the first cat, fox, or stoat that passes that way, and in this manner dozens upon dozens of young pheasants are lost to the shooter.

On most lands some peewits will be found to nest, and remain all spring and summer. These birds should never on any account be disturbed or shot, as they are of the greatest help to the gamekeeper, being the most vigilant of watchmen by day, and even by night when clear and moonlight. They generally confine themselves to one good large field, and should cat, dog, fox stoat, &c., or man make his appearance, they will instantly begin their singular and persistent gyrations, calling "pee-wit, pe-e-e-wit" as loudly as they can squall. The gamekeeper hearing or seeing this should immediately hasten cautiously to the spot to see what is "up." Should the cause of alarm go out of sight, the bird will at once again settle down, and resume his attentions to his mate, who is on the nest somewhere handy.

A keeper may often save himself a lot of trouble, and some walking of a night (particularly when partially cloudy, with dark intervals). There are often times that he cannot see across even a small field. On approaching a gateway to quietly peep through to try and observe what is going on at such times, if he kneels down against the gate-post and places his ear flat against it, pressing it so close that not a particle of air or sound can get in from the outside, in this position (when his ear is well educated) he will readily detect a man's footsteps across a 10-acre field, and hear dog, fox, hare, or rabbit, if they scamper across any part of it. When they move slowly, or a cat steals along, they cannot be detected; but the alarm stamp of a rabbit is always quite prominent. I have often speculated to myself what it is that conveys these impressions to the brain. Is it sound, or is it vibration, or a combination of both? But I can never satisfy myself what it really is. Yet the impressions are so palpable that a practised ear will be able to detect in the darkest night whether it is fox, dog, hare, or rabbit. The two former are the most difficult to distinguish, while the two latter are very distinct; but where several all bolt together, the listener is completely "up a tree." Still, he may be certain of this, that there is something going on that should be investigated. If poachers are talking in a low voice, some words may occasionally be distinctly made out; even a stage whisper the other side of a field will produce a buzzing sensation on the brain. It is a very good plan for a keeper to practise this a bit from time to time in the moonlight, when he can see what is going on, as the eye then assists him in unravelling the different impressions conveyed, and refer each to its proper source.

December 31st 1898

PART TWO

12-BORE 2½-INCH TRUE CYLINDER AT 40 YARDS
Load: 33 grains Smokeless Diamond and 1 1/16 ounce of No. 6
127 Pellets in 30-inch circle

The *Field* Letters

THE SHOOTER OF 1850

Letter of Reminiscence

By publication date, this letter to *The Field* predates the previous section, so it may well be that this sowed the idea of the longer series.

While it is very likely remembered through rose-tinted glasses, nevertheless it captures some of the excitement and satisfaction to be had from hunting pheasants in this way.

SIR – It is really quite refreshing in the present day to find something said in favour of old fashioned sport, and your excellent article quite took me back to my boy days, as in my dear old father's time we always kept a number of – little dogs – beagles and spaniels over which nearly all our best sport was had as the pointers and setters were seldom out except in September. I know nothing in sport more truly enjoyable than a day such as you describe, with one agreeable companion, safe with his gun to take the opposite side of hedge, dingle or dell, with a man to carry the game, and occasionally to get in the end of a hedgerow to prevent the birds running back into covert – three or four brace of cock pheasants, as many couple of rabbits, with a bird or two which offer delicious shots when put up from the sunny side of some gill and knocked over as he passes out, it really makes one's mouth water to write of it; and I do think there is more keen enjoyment and time spent in one such day than in a whole week of battues, with unlimited beaters, unlimited shooters and unlimited slaughter.

Our beagles were expressly trained for this work and excellent they were never passing feather or flick, and were as free from chase as spaniels and less hollered on; but I could never get them to stop either to hand or gun, but some of them retrieved very fairly. I much preferred them to spaniels.

One who has fired some 20,000 trial shots at marks

The Field, October 6th 1888 (Page 495)

It is worthy of note how, on a wild bird shoot, only cocks were shot. Finally, spare a thought for the well-laden keeper on the trek home.

The First Letter

Given the volume of A.J.L.'s contributions to *The Field*, the first letter would have demanded inclusion here, no matter what its content. In the event, we have a wonderfully informative piece, well worth all the effort involved in a trip to the Natural History Museum to gain sight of it.

The content is close to a life-plan, with the home gunmaking and pattern testing as the past and the letter itself – although Lane was mercifully unaware at the time of writing of the mishap that was to befall him – a portent of things to come.

LENGTH OF GUN-BARRELS.- Having lately seen in THE FIELD many letters on the, to me, highly interesting subject, the length of gun-barrels, and as this is a thing on which I have experimented a good deal, I think it right to give your correspondents the benefit of my experiences, and they must take them for what they are worth. I possess sundry doubles, the longest of which is 24 inches, and the shortest 16 inches – the latter a purely experimental pair of barrels; and I propose to forward a trial paper, showing the shooting of each, that your correspondents may judge for themselves as to the shooting of short barrels. I usually try guns at sheets of the Times marked with a central bull's-eye, behind which I place a folded pad of twenty-four strong brown papers, the "penetration column" showing the number of pellets thrown into them and the number going through. The sizes of these are – Times sheet, 24½in. by 18½in.; pad, 10in. by 6in. This pad of brown paper is the best method I know of testing the relative hardness of the shooting, greatly less deceptive than the plate. My experiments lead me to the conclusion that sportsmen using guns of 13 or smaller gauges may please themselves as to length of barrels from 20in. upwards, provided they can get their gunmakers to take the requisite trouble to rebore for shooting. I do this myself, but I find at times barrels get beyond the reach of apparatus not having a boring bench, but only make-shift bits running in a lathe, in which case I despatch them to Squires, of Whitechapel, who charges a very moderate sum, and bores and rebores till I am satisfied. I have never yet found a pair of barrels of 13 or smaller bore spoiled by cutting to this length; larger than this gauge I have not tried. The cutting of a barrel necessarily alters the shooting, as it throws it out of balance by cutting off pro rata so much of the relief forward, and, in nineteen cases out of twenty, alters it for the worse, but the shooting is generally pretty easily got back by "tickling" at the muzzle. The position inside of short barrels that I have usually found answer best, is as near a perfect cylinder as possible, to within three inches or so of the muzzle, from thence slightly relieved. Barrels thus bored I find usually shoot better as they get foul, whereas, those opened behind, almost as universally shoot worse. This plan, however, cannot always be carried out in practice. My usual mode of proceeding is to slightly alter the cupping of the breech till the barrel shoots strong enough, then relieving the muzzle until the charge is sufficiently kept together; beginning with about two inches down to four or five, or even more. Failing this, as a last resource, opening a little behind. I have generally found the elliptically (not the merely semi-circularly) cupped patent breech shoot hardest. My experience of coned breeches has been but small, but what I have seen has not prepossessed me in their favour. I may add, that I have, within the last five-and-twenty years, tried some hundreds of barrels, and by most of the crack makers, but have, in most instances, found the short barrels quite equal to the long, and, in many instances, far exceeding the common average of guns. As regards recoil; weight, weight, is the thing. If two guns, a long and short, are of equal weights, in nineteen cases out of twenty, so far as my experiences go, it is considerably less in the short; taking, too, no equal loads but that best suiting each. But the manner of boring also affects this. I think it will be found guns opened behind usually recoil more than those that are cylindrical towards the breech, but it must be admitted that short guns are more apt to jump than long ones, but it is very seldom that guns that labour much shoot well. The reason that most gunmakers object to short guns, I apprehend is, that they frequently give more trouble in getting them up to the required standard, but it can be done if they will take the trouble. My only excuse for troubling you with so lengthy a communication is that, to some of your readers (like myself) a short, light gun is "everything," and it may be an inducement to such sportsmen to carry out their object more boldly, and I think few men who have enjoyed the luxury of a short, light, handy gun for a season, would be induced to go back to the conventional thirty inches; the quickness and accuracy with which an object may be sighted with a 20-inch as against a 30-inch pair of barrels is perfectly marvellous. I can only say, further, that I shall, at any time, be happy to show you, or any of your correspondents, my guns, and what they will do, and give any further information in my power privately.

One who has fired some 10,000 trial shots at marks

P.S. With regard to "Indoctus's" remark about the wind, he will find a high wind affect the shooting of a good gun either in force and garnish to the extent of some 20 per cent at forty paces, and a bad one much more. Nor am I surprised at what he says of No. 4 shot. It is a curious fact that, with all the barrels I have tried, I have not known one in twenty that would throw them tolerably through otherwise good guns. Can any of your correspondents account for this? I imagine that I have never tried a bore that they really fit.

The Field, March 31st 1860 (Page 251)

TRIAL PAPER

SHOT	LOAD DRS OZ	DISTANCE 30 40 50 RIGHT	PENETRATION	OBSERVATIONS	DISTANCE 30 40 50	PENETRATION	OBSERVATIONS
\multicolumn{8}{c}{13 GAUGE 24 INCH BARRELS WEIGHT 5LBS 12OZ}
No. 6	2¾ 1¼	- 104 -	19 in, 5 thro	Held too high	- 119 -	Pad swelled	Very even
		- 93 -	18 in, 10 thro	Very even	- 110 -	24 in, 13 thro	Beautiful
		- - 70	15 in, 9 thro	Capital centre	- - 72	10 in, 7 thro	Very even
\multicolumn{8}{c}{18 GAUGE 22 INCH BARRELS WEIGHT 5LBS 8OZ}
No. 6	2½ 1⅛	- 68 -	11 in, 4 thro	Very fair	- 104 -	9 in, 5 thro	Good
		- 92 -	10 in, 6 thro	Fairly even	- 89 -	16 in, 12 thro	Good
		- - 74	15 in, 9 thro	Very good	- - 61	7 in, 2 thro	Good
\multicolumn{8}{c}{25 GAUGE 16 INCH BARRELS WEIGHT ABOUT 5 LBS}
No. 6	2 1	111 - -	18 in, 7 thro	Pretty even	82 - -	9 in, 3 thro	Fair
		84 - -		Rather patchy	93 - -	10 in, 3 thro	Fair
\multicolumn{8}{c}{16 GAUGE 20 INCH BARRELS WEIGHT 5LBS 11½ OZ}
No. 6	2½ 1⅛	- 70 -	19 in, 7 thro	Very fair	- 93 -	14 in, 12 thro	Pretty even
		- 61 -	9 in, 2 thro	Very fair	- 85 -	15 in, 9 thro	Good
		- - 47	5 in, 2 thro	Very fair	- - 58	9 in, 5 thro	Good

It is regretted that pages of *The Times* were used as pattern sheets, because the format differs from all other published tests and so comparison with them is not possible.

While Walsh is completely accurate with his observation of the variable results for penetration obtained from paper pads, a more helpful comment would have been to suggest that, if a gun with longer barrels had been tried on the same day, with the same loads and against the same pads, then, while an absolute value would still not have been obtained, a ratio would have emerged and this would have been of real, practical use and interest.

The Inventions of A.J. Lane

So far in this narrative, we have seen many examples of contrivances and creations produced by Arthur Lane. This section is concerned with what could well be termed more serious inventions, one of which was pursued as far as a patent. In passing, it is perhaps worthy of remarking that these are the known inventions. I would be very surprised if there were not many others that did not get beyond the sketch-on-the-back-of-an-envelope stage.

Three innovations are mentioned at various points – the platinum-lined percussion nipple, the 'shot concentrator' and a breech loading rifle.

With his patent No. 1536 of 1858, Arthur Lane was frankly wasting his money, but we should be grateful that he did, because it gives us another insight into his career.

The following is an excerpt from the patent, in fact the great part of the provisional specification. This was a description composed by the patent agent, in this case Alexander Prince of 4, Trafalgar Square, London, but as it must have been based on a description written by A.J.L. and presumably approved by him, it is as close as we can now get to a description in his own words.

> NOW KNOW YE, that I, the said Arthur James Lane, do hereby declare the nature of the said Invention, and in what manner the same is to be performed, to be particularly described and ascertained in and by the following statement thereof (that is to say):

My Invention relates to certain improvements in breech-loading fire-arms, and is designed for the purpose of rendering the same more efficient than heretofore; and the principal features of novelty of my said Invention are a peculiar arrangement of mechanism for bringing the barrel of the gun out of a straight line with the breech thereof when loading, and securely holding it in that position during the discharge of the contents of the gun. And in order to point out in what respects the construction of breech-loading fire-arms, according to my said Invention, differs from that of other breech-loading fire-arms as heretofore constructed, I now proceed to describe generally the principle of construction of my said Invention as follows, that is to say:- Instead of connecting the barrels of breech-loading fire-arms to the breech thereof by screwing or other of the modes heretofore practised for effecting the same, I proceed as follows:- I first connect or hinge the breech-piece of the gun to the iron work of the stock thereof (technically termed the break-off) which receives the breech, by means of a screw pivot or pin, upon which the breech moves freely. I then proceed to connect the barrel of the gun to the aforesaid break-off, by attaching to or forming upon the breech end of the barrel and at each side thereof a bar of metal, through which a hole is made or connecting the same to the said break-off by screws or other convenient means. And an important feature in my said Invention consists in arranging the before-mentioned centres or fulcra upon which the breech and barrel move, and by which such said parts are brought together and separated from each other in such a manner that the fulcra or centres of motion are not in the same plane; which I effect in the following manner, that is to say, I place the centre of motion of the breech-piece in a line with the centre of the bore of such said breech-piece, and I place the centre of motion of the aforesaid barrel as much above and behind the centre of motion of the breech-piece as is necessary for imparting a slight excentric (sic) movement to the barrel, and thus to bring the breech end of the barrel into close and forced contact with the end of the before-mentioned hinged breech-piece; which I effect by imparting to the aforesaid breech-piece and barrel the compound movement above stated.

All that can be added to this description is that the chamber contains a tooth or cutter to open the paper cartridge, which had to be loaded powder end first.

A point that needs to be raised is the absolute necessity of removing any smouldering remnants of the case from the chamber before the next round is inserted. Failure to do this would have resulted in a very nasty fright at best, at worst a potentially serious accident.

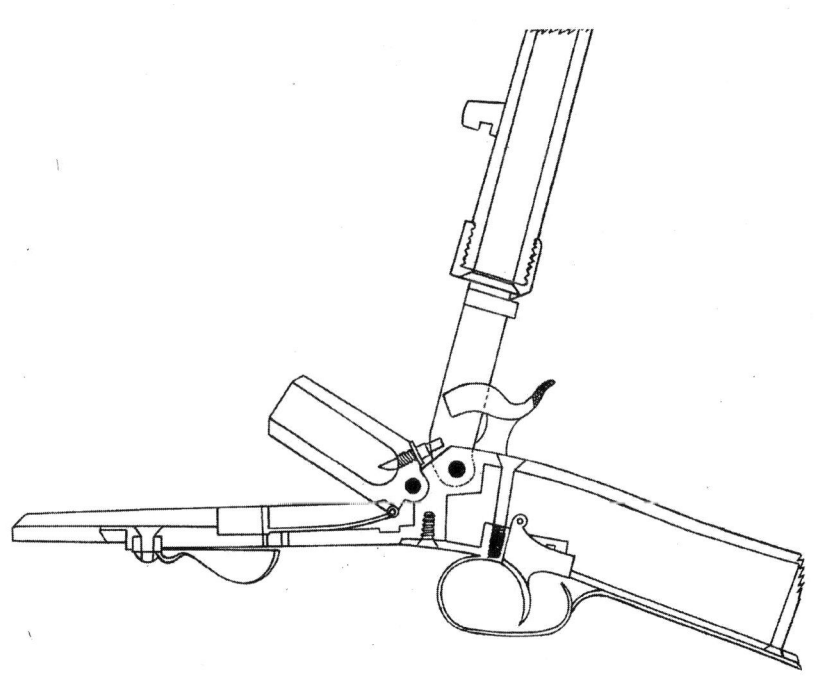

Patent No. 1536 of 1858

There are no other known claimants to the idea of the lined nipple and it remained on offer in suppliers' catalogues for most of the end of the 19th century. That said, they are not widely encountered, possibly because unlined nipples were inexpensive and readily exchanged on a gun.

By contrast, the shot concentrator was a far more useful contrivance. Until it was made redundant by choke-bored barrels, it offered a practical way of increasing the range of a shotgun. Moreover, it had the advantage that it was something that lent itself to home manufacture. Consisting of nothing more complex than a cardboard cylinder open at both ends, or, more easily made, a roll of gummed paper, all that was needed was that it should fit reasonably well in the bore of the gun.

Arthur Lane left us an account of his experiences in the shape of a letter published in *The Field* of March 6th 1880, which reads:

CONCENTRATORS AND SCHULTZE POWDER

SIR, As I was the original inventor of the paper-cylinder concentrators, having used them for many years before they were brought out by Mr. Lancaster, and given them and the formula for making them to many brother sportsmen (among them your esteemed correspondent "Indoctus") I may be able to give Col. Whyte some information respecting them.

I gave up the use of them when I took to breech loaders, as I found they almost invariably split open in the cone immediately in front of the chamber, in which case they were worse than useless, being an absolute detriment to the shooting. I never knew but one breech loader in which they were any good, and that was a gun I have mentioned before in your columns which I had made with an abrupt shoulder at the end of the chamber. In this they did very well.

I think Col. Whyte's must be made of very bad soft paper to blow to fragments as he mentions, or it may be possible that he has not looked far enough afield for them, as if they answer at all, they travel from twelve to twenty five yards from the muzzle, and I hardly need say the further they go the better will be the results.

The best form I have found for them is to cut the concentrators the exact length to hold the whole charge of shot (not a pellet more or less) so that when the top wadding is put on, there may be neither shaking nor compression. Used in this way, you get about the same in both pattern and penetration at 55 yards that you do with some gun with loose charges at 40; but they should be confined to the second barrel as they render the gun useless at close quarters, the disc covered at 20 to 25 yards not being more than eight or nine inches to a foot, and frequently less. They should be an easy fit in the bore, but not stuck enough to pass without the weight of the ramrod on them. They are singularly irregular in their action in different guns. In some of my own they have exceeded the results given, while in others they were quite useless; for which I could never find out a reason, in the boring or otherwise.

I have never fired one out of a choke – indeed in very light guns I should have feared to do so, as if tight enough to be of any use they would add a fearful strain at the muzzle, and if slack enough pass the choke without injury, would be almost certain to split in the barrels; and even if one should occasionally pass the choke intact, I think nothing would be gained as all the benefit from the choking would be lost; and that arising from a concentrator at its best, cannot compare for a moment, especially in the important item of regularity in the shooting with those of the choke.

One who has fired some 20,000 trial shots at marks

P.S. If I can give any further information or assistance to Col. Whyte I should be most pleased to do so.

THE FIELD, March 6th 1880 (Page 270)

Interestingly, there is another Arthur Lane letter published in *The Field* of August 10th 1895, which gives a more complete picture of the evolution of the concentrator. Part of this reads:

> The most successful mode of preventing the friction in the barrel was a spiral spring of hard brass wire about five or six coils and an easy fit in the calibre. This caused a very much better pattern at all ranges but still a great number of pellets were crushed out of shape.
>
> Subsequently I hit on the idea of making a brown paper cylinder a close fit in the bore; this I cut off to the exact length occupied by the charge intended.

Yet again we have a contribution born of hard experience. What is curious about these findings is that they appear to fly in the face of other contemporary experiences.

It will be realised that, at the 1876 trial of cylinder versus choke guns at live pigeon trap shooting, the cylinders beat the chokes, but the following year the chokes won. In the first trial concentrators were permitted, but in the second they were excluded.

Walsh in *The Modern Sportsman's Gun & Rifle* records trials he had made with his Westley Richards breech loader, in which concentrators increased both pattern and penetration by about 25%. The explanation of this apparent anomaly may be that A.J.L. was using sleeves which encased the full length of the shot charge, while the Lancaster version only gave partial coverage.

A.J. Lanes's Investigation of the Ball and Shotgun

In *The Field* of April 20th 1889, a correspondent who called himself "Gordon Setter" had a letter published in which he enquired if a cheaper equivalent of a Lancaster "Colindian" might be found in a cylinder-bored gun adapted to fire ball cartridges.

The Colindian was the response made by H.A.A. Thorn (aka "Charles Lancaster"), proprietor of the firm of the same name,

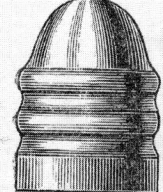

CHARLES LANCASTER

Begs most respectfully to draw the attention of Sportsmen to his

LATEST GUN.

As supplied to H.I.M.'s Government of India and many well-known Sportsmen in all parts of the World.

THE GUN TO TAKE ABROAD IS

"THE COLINDIAN,"

(TRADE MARK REGISTERED).

A Non-fouling, smooth, oval bore Rifled Gun, shooting elongated conical shaped Bullets, accurately, from 20 to 100 yards, and shot of all sizes, as well as a modified choke-bore, and which has neither grooved rifling nor choke-boring to offer resistance to shot or ball, and consequently prevents leading, fouling and undue recoil.

These Guns are accurately sighted at 50 and 100 yards. Loads—3drs. of powder and "Express" bullet 765grs. (1¾ oz.). 4drs. of powder and "Express" bullet, with steel plug.

Bullet.

PRICES.

Top Lever Snap Action Double-barrel B.L. Hammer Gun, with Rebounding Locks, Hammers below the line of sight.

£27 for Cash with Order only.   Credit Price **£30.**

Top Lever Snap Action Double-barrel B.L. Hammerless Gun, with Automatic Trigger Safety and Blocking Safeties for the Mainsprings, easily taken to pieces for cleaning, highly praised for its strength and simple action by the Editor of "The Field," &c., &c.

For description of Mechanism see "Colonial Quality" Illustrated Lists.

£36 for Cash with Order only.   Credit Price **£40.**   Section of Bullet.

THE ABOVE ARE OF GOOD SOUND QUALITY, PLAINLY FINISHED WITHOUT ENGRAVING.

Special Guns of Highest Finish and Engraving from £10 extra, made to Order.

These Guns are 12-bore only, and chambered for Eley's ordinary 12-bore central fire Paper Cases, and are about 7½ lbs. weight.

CAUTION!!!

C.L. begs to inform purchasers of partly or wholly Rifled Guns for Ball and Shot, that not one of his has failed to pass the legal proof-house tests by bulging or bursting at the muzzle.

These Guns may be tested at C.L.'s Private Range before purchase.

A Sportsman having one of the above Guns, and a "Double-Barrel Express Rifle," is fully equipped for Sport in any part of the World.

to the commercial challenge posed by the Holland & Holland "Paradox", in which George Fosbery's system of a rifled choke had, for practical purposes, doubled the accurate range of bullets fired from a gun which would also effectively fire bird shot.

This enhanced performance also enabled the vendors to charge enhanced prices for their guns. The Fosbery patent, for which Messrs. Holland & Holland paid the inventor a guinea per barrel, enabled them to sell what was essentially a £15 hammer gun for £35.

Since the oval bore used in the Colindian was in the public domain, that is not protected by a patent, the premium that could be charged was less. In addition, the Colindian did not handle shot as well as the Paradox, but nevertheless in 1889 a basic grade Colindian was priced about a third higher than an equivalent shotgun - £27 as against £20.

In the very next issue of *The Field*, that of April 27th 1889, on page 577, we find this most interesting response from Arthur Lane:

> SIR, - I shall with great pleasure give your correspondent "Gordon Setter" any information I can on this subject, but I must commence by stating that, I have plenty of cylinders and also rifles in my gun rack, I have never fired ball from a choke, considering it could never by satisfactory, as years ago I satisfied myself that the final direction of a bullet from a smoothbore depends entirely upon how it conducts itself during its passage through the last few inches of the barrel; and I think that, as the choke is within an inch of the muzzle, where the ball would meet with a sudden shock, it would be eminently calculated to divert it in some direction out of the line of sight. Moreover, I am inclined to think the process would be attended with some considerable risk – I do not mean to the shooter, but to the weapon. I have always found a chamois leather patch indispensable in using ball with any accuracy from a

smoothbore. Now, should this leather get tightly jammed round the ball, I think it would be extremely likely to take out a part or even the whole of the choke in its passage through it. Such has been and is still my view; but I should be sorry to set it up against such a high experimental authority as Mr. W.W. Greener.

Many years ago I tried a number of experiments with different forms of rifle bullets from smoothbores. With some of these a good spin was obtained, with fair accuracy at moderate distances, but all more or less uncertain, and they could not hold a candle to even a very moderate rifle at longer ranges. In my opinion, the best practice from a smooth-bore is to be got with a spherical bullet with a tail. The preparation is rather troublesome and occupies some time, but the accuracy amply repays it. The bullet should be of a size that will roll slowly and steadily without a check the entire length of the barrel both ways. In casting, care must be taken that there is no air bubble in the bullet, as this will inevitably produce a wild shot. The first three or four bullets in casting – *i.e.*, until the mould has got hot – will almost certainly have these bubbles, and should consequently be dropped in the melting ladle. Each bullet should be weighed against one of known accurate weight, and all light ones rejected. The bullets should then be drilled, and a tail about 6in. long, of medium-size pack thread, or a bit of trout line, added. Drive a wedge of tough wood into the bullet beside the string, and cut both off together. Having done this, place them in an oven, and while they are heating cut some chamois leather patches with four leaves, much in the shape like the flower of a single tulip assumes just before falling, except that the tip of the leaves should be a little more pointed, and just the size to easily cover the bullet. Place these on the bullet, and draw the point of each leaf down to the twine and then pass round them three turns of a fine silk and one "half hitch." If tied tighter than this, the patch will cling to the bullet too long after leaving the gun. The bullets thus covered should be dropped into a bowl of hot grease, consisting of one part beeswax and two parts tallow; hang them up by the tail to cool. In loading, put a thick felt wadding over the powder, drop the tail straight into the barrel, and then push down the bullet firmly on the wadding; but put no wadding over it – the grease will hold it in its place. For a breechloader, put a card grease-proof wad next the powder, then a thick felt, then coil the tail into the cartridge case, and press the bullet firmly down; then pour sufficient hot grease on the top to entirely cover it level over; not wadding on top; do not turn down or crimp the case. I generally found less powder than that used in the gun for shot would give the most accurate results with a smoothbore – say, nearly ½ dr. less in a 12-bore, or ¼ dr. less in smaller gauges. Thus loaded, a 6in. "bull" may be struck an indefinite number of times at 60 yards, and very fair shooting can be got at double this distance; but beyond this not much must be expected from a smoothbore.

I do not think stout barrel are at all necessary, as I believe the strain on the barrel by a round bullet treated as above is considerably less than that produced by an ordinary charge (for the bore) of small shot, on account of there being no jamming together to produce inordinate friction; but if an elongated, conical, and consequently much heavier projectile be used, the case is very different, as more powder is required, and the resistance at starting greatly increased, and stout barrels become necessary. But I may here remark that I do not believe in conical bullets out of a smoothbore. No spin being imparted by the barrel, they are very apt to speedily upset in their flight, and their course then becomes very erratic, so that no reliance whatever can be placed upon them even at very moderate distances. Moreover, what with the increased weight of lead and the greater charge of powder required to obtain a proper velocity, the recoil in an ordinary double barrel becomes intolerable enough to preclude the possibility of putting in the other barrel effectively with sufficient quickness, should such a contingency arise and be required; whereas the spherical balls go as "easy as a glove," and short barrels (24in.) throw their bullets quite as accurately as long ones.

For close quarters such as "Gordon Setter" describes with his adventure with the panther, I think a man might face such a dangerous brute as fearlessly with his double gun loaded as above as with a rifle. For my own part, I think I should prefer it; as the gun, being much lighter and handier than the rifle, can be brought to bear much more quickly on the object, and up to 20 yards would, I think, have the advantage. Rifles at this distance often shoot high, and a bullet intended to go between the eyes of a charging animal might take effect in the back, when, if the spine were not struck, the consequences would probably be serious. It must be no joke to be mauled by panther or tiger.

One who has fired over 20,000 trial shots at marks

The idea of a "ball with a tail" is one of those that has reappeared in several guises and locations throughout the long story of ballistics. What we cannot know is if Lane was aware of these earlier essays or whether he rediscovered it independently. It works because it inhibits and perhaps even eliminates what is known today as the 'Robins-Magnus' effect. This can be described in a simplistic way as the deviation in the path of a spherical projectile which is launched with a spin on an axis at right angles to its line of flight. In recent times, this phenomenon has attracted interest because of its importance in various ball games.

In the case of a gun or musket, this rotation is induced when the ball, not being a perfect fit in the bore, grazes one side of the barrel immediately prior to its exit. Thus a spin is set up, which, in the case of a naked ball, is enhanced by the propellant gases escaping through the gap on the other side. As Arthur Lane points out, accuracy is also improved by effective wadding and by use of a patched ball.

From our present perspective, what is more important is the question of why Arthur Lane was experimenting in this way? None of the writings yet discovered make any reference to shooting anything larger than a Brown Hare. There are, however, mentions of visits to Scotland – perhaps this is the clue?

NOTE: For a much more erudite and fuller explanation of the Robins-Magnus effect in small arms, the reader is urged to consult the following works of David Harding:

Lead Shot of the English Civil War, a Radical Study
Small Arms of the East India Company, 1600 – 1856, Vol III

The Field Trials and the Choke Bore

To understand the phenomenon of A.J. Lane and his massive commitment to the exterior ballistics of the sporting shotgun, we need to put him into the context of the age in which he lived. The middle decades of the 19th century saw advances in practically every aspect of technology, often led by progress in measurement and scientific understanding, which took the place of the empiricism of earlier times.

So it was that, in 1858, in an attempt to resolve a controversy which had developed in the correspondence columns of the paper concerning the shooting powers of the new breech loading shotguns in comparison with the old muzzle loader, the editorial staff of *The Field* led by the great J.H. Walsh, organised a trial, which attempted to produce a scientific answer to the problem. By almost any measure you care to apply, this approach was a success and, for the rest of the century, trials of all sorts were a valuable feature of *The Field*'s coverage of shooting matters.

The first trial was held on 9th and 10th April, 1858, at Ashburnham Park, Chelsea to compare the shooting of muzzle loading guns with the upcoming breech loaders. A second, follow-up event was held the following year on 4th and 5th July at Hornsey Wood House.

What is relevant to this study is that these trials were relatively small affairs. In the write-up on the second trial, it is noted that the attendees were the competitors, some other members of the gun trade and "a few ardent lovers of the trigger." It would be difficult to better that phrase as a description of Arthur Lane and we learn from the biography in *The Sporting Mirror* that this was the first trial he had attended, but then he was present at all the subsequent events.

A third trial took place on 22nd and 23rd May, 1866, at The Lillie Arms, Old Brompton, this time to compare the "comparative merits of modern breech loaders."

As an aside, the list of guns tested gives a revealing snap-shot of the evolution of the sporting gun. Both pin and centre fire guns were represented and even one muzzle loader, along with all sorts of patent actions and, while most had Damascus barrels, there was one with steel barrels.

Today we are apt to take the choke for granted but, to read of all the effort that was expended in the earlier part of the 19th century to achieve denser shot patterns, is to realise that the choke must have been like the philosopher's stone.

The origin of the choke bore is obscure and is likely to remain so because proving early 19th century claims and stories is now impossible. What is fact is that, in *The Field* of December 5th 1874, William W. Greener caused the following advertisement to be published:

> W.W.G. is now prepared to manufacture guns to order that will put on an average of 210 pellets, with 12-bores, weighing under 7¼ lbs., with a charge of 3 drachms powder, and 1⅛oz. of No. 6 shot; and over that weight, 220 pellets; 10-bore guns, weighing 9 to 9½lbs., with a charge of only 4 drachms of powder and 1¼oz., No. 6 shot, an average of 240 pellets. Closer shooting may be obtained if desired, and the penetration is also one-third greater. By using only 2¼ drachms of powder, better pattern and penetration can be obtained than from other guns with 3 drachms of powder, and with much less recoil.

It is not to be wondered at that this provoked considerable scepticism and Arthur Lane' beautifully crafted letter of disbelief appeared in *The Field* of January 1st 1875.

> SIR,-I read with great interest your report of the extraordinary shooting powers of these guns, but I observe the trial was made under cover. Will they do as much in the open air? I doubt it. I have been told by first-rate gunsmiths that they cannot depend on the shooting of guns so tried; and my own experience, though small, of trial shots fired under cover, fully confirms this. It is clear some of the most trying atmospheric influences in modifying the flight of a charge of shot are wholly avoided in the perfect stillness of a gallery. It would be a great thing if you could lay before your readers a properly authenticated trial under the ordinary condition of a day's shooting. Again, will they hold their shooting? Many of these schemes do well for a time, and soon go off, as has been the case with several submitted to me for trial. Mr Greener's great reputation is a practical guarantee for this, but the true one can only be time and hard work. I have tried the shooting some years ago of several of Mr Greener's guns, and always found them up to or above the average.
>
> *One who has fired upwards of 20,000 trial shots at marks*

This controversy was an obvious cue for another Field trial, in fact two, one to test the shooting of the boring, the other resilience of the bore.

The shooting trial, "The Field Gun Trial of 1875", was held at Wimbledon on the ground of the All England Croquet Club, with Arthur Lane as one of the committee appointed by Mr. Walsh to assist in running the trial. In this, William Greener made good his claim and won the all important Class 2 for 'Guns of 12 gauge and under of any boring, weight not to exceed 7¼lbs charge of shot 1⅛', for which he was awarded a silver cup, value 40 guineas. He also won Class 1 for 8 bores and Class 4 for 20 bores.

There is no mention of Arthur Lane's involvement in the second trial, the so-called Wear and Tear Trial in which two and a half thousand cartridges were fired from each of three guns to test the durability of the choke.

All of the evidence points to Arthur being hugely impressed by the choke bore and he became a lifelong advocate of its use. In the shorter term, he offered a prize to try and solve the controversy that, as in the case of most significant discoveries, had arisen concerning the true inventor. Thus in The Field of April 17th 1875 we find the following letter.

THE NEW CLOSE-SHOOTING SYSTEM OF BORING
PRIZE OF £10.10S. FOR INVENTOR OR FIRST USER

SIR,-The late letters and articles in *The Field* relative to the extraordinary power of these guns having given rise to much discussion as to the origin of this boring, and there being great reason to doubt its being truly an American invention – for, although I believe Americans claim to have used it in 1870, and that it was not known here until about 1873, yet several respectable makers assert that it was in fact copied by them from English-bored guns – I think some effort should be made to settle this question, so as to let the real inventor (or first user in this country) get the credit fairly due to him; and, the plan being no longer a trade secret, I am induced to offer, and will give, a prize cup (value £10. 10s.) or the money to the English gun maker who can satisfactorily prove either his being the original inventor or the first user in this country of the system; and I hope your committee on the approaching gun trials will kindly undertake to examine the evidence and award the prize.

I think this will prevent an injustice being done to the originator (whosoever he may be) of a highly valuable invention, and will be acceptable to all shooters.

I beg to append short rules for those intending to compete:

1st. All evidence to be documentary; patents, registrations, descriptive drawings, &c., to be verified in all important points by statutory declarations; or

2nd. Production of guns bored on the principle in the hands of gentlemen of undoubted respectability, certified by the owners as to date of make, and that they have not been re-bored or altered, and also by statutory declaration of the makers.

All evidence to be examined, and prize awarded by *The Field* Gun Trial Committee, or by the Editor. In the event of any difficulty arising as to the boring or description of system, that Mr Purdey, Mr Lancaster, or some other magnate in the gun trade, not claiming, be requested to act as referee.

All papers to be sent in to *The Field* office on or before the 26th day of April next, addressed to the Editor, and endorsed "Claim for prize for invention of new close-shooting system of boring shot guns."

One who has fired upwards of 20,000 trial shots at marks.

In the event, by virtue of his patent No. 1501 of 1866, which claims a muzzle bored one size smaller than the bore, the Newcastle-upon-Tyne gunmaker, William R. Pape was able to win the competition and took the cash instead of the cup.

From a consideration of the career of Arthur Lane, there is another important aspect to this story of the introduction of the choke bore. As will be seen in Appendix I and elsewhere in this study, Arthur wrote a group of four letters to *The Field* in early 1875. In these we see a precedent for the letters and articles that were to appear later in the century.

For medical reasons that we can now only guess at, sometime in 1878, as a result of a haemorrhage in the eye ball, Arthur lost the sight in his right eye permanently. Since the overwhelming bulk of his writing post-dates this life-changing mishap, compelling logic suggests that the writing provided an outlet for his energies and without it his story would never have been recorded.

Arthur Lane also served on the committee of the 1879 trial, which compared the shooting of 12, 16 and 20 bore guns, at which, to general surprise, a 16 bore emerged victorious.

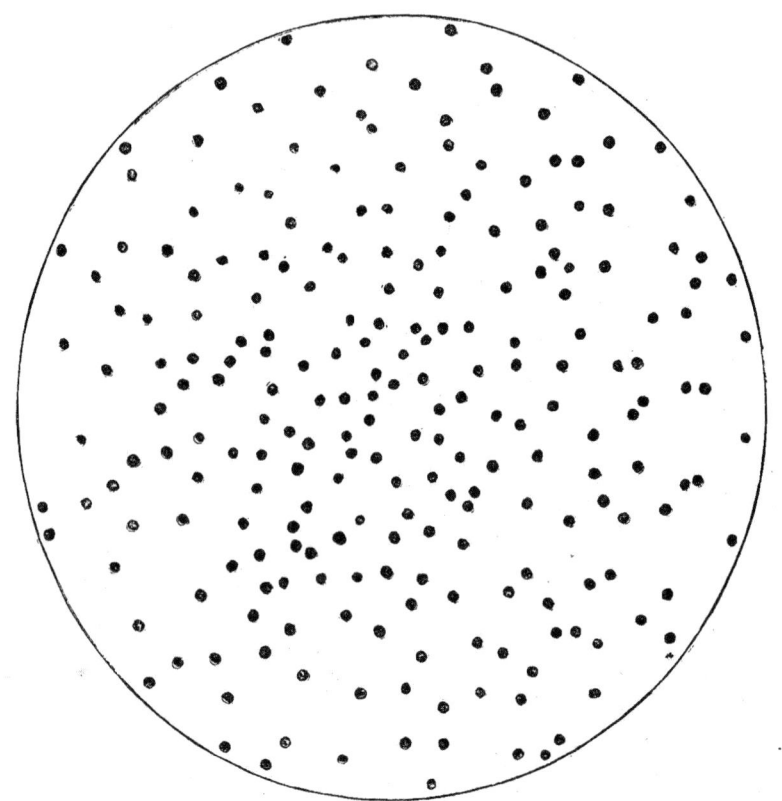

Fac-simile of the Shooting of a W. W. Greener Gun with Schultze Powder and No. 6 Shot.

Pattern reproduced from *Modern Shotguns* by W.W. Greener. Claimed to be a photographic copy of the pattern made by the Greener gun, No. 19,304, made for the Schultze Company; load, 42 grains of Schultze and 1⅛ oz. No. 6 shot.

Weston's of Brighton

When Arthur Lane moved to Brighton, it is inconceivable that he did not seek out the local gunmaker and so he would have come into contact with Weston's. In the 1870s, the firm traded as C. & H. Weston, presumably a partnership between Charles and Herbert Weston, who were the successors to one William Weston who first appears in the Brighton street directories in 1825.

This information was gleaned from Nigel Brown's magnum opus, *British Gunmakers, Volume II*, which also lists other Weston's trading in the area and gun and clock makers as far back as a certain Abraham Weston, who was recorded in Lewes in 1676.

The relationship, (if any!), between all of these traders is, of course, a matter of speculation, but a wonderful subject for a study project. What it could mean is that, when Arthur first stepped into the shop, the business could have claimed foundation some 200 years earlier.

Regrettably, Arthur has left us no record of any oral tradition which might have existed. All we have in his published letters are favourable comments on guns sold and the professional knowledge of the proprietors.

While living in Brighton, Arthur's pattern testing continued. To date no record of a Weston shooting ground has emerged, so the one mention of a shooting ground in the letters is thought to refer to Sheepcote Valley, where the volunteers had a range.

C. & H. WESTON,
GUNMAKERS AND ATHLETIC OUT-FITTERS,
NEW ROAD, BRIGHTON, AND HIGH-STREET, HAILSHAM,

THE LARGEST, CHEAPEST, AND BEST ASSORTED STOCK OF GUNS, CARTRIDGES and all other Shooting Requisites in the South of England.

The BRIGHTON CARTRIDGE is the embodiment of the best selected Smokeless Powder; finest materials and the most accurate loading; 10s. 6d. per 100; Best Cartridges possibly to be made.

Our "SPECIAL" CARTRIDGE is the best value ever offered. All English Cases. Once tried always used.

Black Powder, 6s. 6d.; Smokeless, 8s. per 100.

This illustration is based on a newspaper advertisement in which the ink had bled to a degree which seriously impaired the legibility and it has been reconstructed on the computer.

A.J. Lane – Shotgun Ballistician

It is the work that Arthur Lane did on shotgun ballistics that sets him apart. While he made no great discoveries and nothing is named after him, his work rewards attention for the simple fact that he appreciated fully the importance of the quality of the pattern. This in contrast with so much that is written on shotgun performance, where it is only the pellet count which seems to matter. Conversely, a corps of experience exists where a fortuitous combination of gun and load give consistent, good performance, far more satisfying than a series of spectacular kills, wounded birds and inexplicable misses, which inevitably result from poor pattern performance.

In this context, a letter published in *The Field* of May 1st 1897 demands inclusion:

20,000 SHOTS AND NO. 5 SHOT.

SIR: For many years past many of us have no doubt wondered who that interesting and instructive writer to The Field was who adopts the pseudonym of "20,000 Shots". Personally the mystery has been solved by this kindly and good old sportsman paying me a visit to test the relative powers of 26in and 30in barrels with different loads. Few young men would have travelled 200 miles – as he did – on purpose, and when I mention that he is many years past the three score years and ten, it will be realised how ready he is to help brother sportsmen – travelling as far as he did for one entire stranger. Full of sporting anecdotes and fond of guns as when he was able to handle them in the masterly way he did a few years ago, makes him a most engaging companion. So keen is our old friend that he sat up every night until midnight loading cartridges for the next day. I wonder how many young men would take this trouble even to test their own gun. The result was that he completely converted me from No. 6 and 7 shot to No. 5. Both guns - viz 30in by Green of Cheltenham and 26in by Ford of Birmingham - made for better pattern with No. 5 shot than with 6 or 7. For twenty years I have only used the two latter as I feared the open pattern of large shot, but I am now fully convinced that a gun bored for No. 5 and shooting that size well, is the gun to have. We know No. 5 is a lot quicker than 6 or 7 and would therefore often give us the extra bit we are behind our game, and admit of long shots, which are often necessary in wild country, and at short ranges No. 5 puts less lead in. The 26in barrels shot as well, if not better than 30in, even up to 60 yards. I am sure all who know "20,000 Shots" or who have read his letters to The Field, will join me in wishing him many more years of health and happiness, and if anyone is fortunate enough to get a gun talk with him, they will look back to it with infinite pleasure.

Convert to No. 5 shot and short barrels.

It is worthy of note that, in 1897, A.J.L. was eighty three years old. The great pity is that we do not know who the letter writer was or where he lived.

As recorded in his autobiography, the seeds of his lifelong interest were sown early and the vital lesson learned of the link between quality of pattern and weight of game bag.

The tenacity with which this quest was followed is a theme running through the next section. Remarkably, all this work was undertaken largely at his own expense – a true amateur in the great Victorian tradition.

Modern Gun Powders

The article *Modern Gun Powders,* published in the magazine of May 1882, is a splendid example of the value and importance of *The Sporting Mirror* to this study, not least because it catalogues the volume of work undertaken to elucidate the value of Schultze powder, which accounted for a sizeable proportion of the famous 20,000 shots, indeed probably half of them, because the change of nom de plume from 10,000 to 20,000 shots occurred about the time Lane's mammoth project was undertaken.

The date quoted – "1868 or 1869" – is intriguing. If correct this would coincide with the founding of the Schultze Company in 1868. Lane getting such good results is at variance with the account of *The Field* Explosives Trial of 1878 and how, after this, Walsh claimed to have devised a mode of loading that revolutionised the performance of the powder.

We cannot know now the explanation for these facts, but a serious failure in communication seems plausible.

In a lighter vein, notice the history of the nickname bestowed on him by his contemporaries.

THE DISCOVERY OF GUNPOWDER

*Five times a century have flown
Since Master Schwartz, monk of Cologne
Of guns and powder claim'd th'invention
Strange matters for a monk's attention.*

Remarks on Shooting, W. Watts, 2nd ed. London 1839

MODERN GUN POWDERS

THERE IS PROBABLY no accessory to the splendid sport of shooting, which has improved more than gunpowder during the last forty or fifty years. The time is well within the recollection of the writer when, really and truly, there was but *one sporting powder* – it is true that the different makers issued powders of various brands, such as "triple strong," "best sporting," "single," "double," and "triple seal," &c., &c. These powders varied slightly in strength, cleanness, and hardness, and undoubtedly some were a trifle better than others, but, inasmuch as they were all of nearly one uniformly fine grain, they may be virtually considered really as amounting to only one powder. And in this same granulation may be said to lie the gist of the matter, as this and the shape mainly controls the rapidity of combustion, a point of vital importance in the shooting to be got out of a gun.

If recollection serves, the first innovation was the introduction, by the Messrs. Hall, of the diamond grain, and a great improvement it was. Then came a coarser, or No. 2 grain – a vast step in the right direction. Then there appeared to be a lull for some considerable time. Ultimately the sizes of the grain went on increasing up to Nos. 6 and 8; the larger, though, were for rifles and heavy bores, and thence up to the enormous pebble and cube powders of the modern artillerist, but with this we have nothing to do here.

That this steady increase in the grain of sporting powders has been of immense advantage to the shooter there can be no question, but – there is always a but! – there can be equally no doubt it can be carried too far! For this shooters have to thank themselves, and themselves only. The powder-makers originally brought out their large grain powder for rifles, but it was the shooters who applied them to their shot-guns; and as there are comparatively few men who will take the trouble, or perhaps have the time, to work out long exhaustive experiments so as to actually prove results, they were adopted too hastily, because they found the guns shot pleasantly and with less recoil, which is an undoubted fact, inasmuch as where there is less force exerted forward there is naturally less reaction, and the large grains required a heavier load. And it may be taken as Q.e.d., that ninety-nine guns out of every hundred will make better shooting with powder of about No. 4 grain than with the larger sizes. A 20-bore gun will often do better with a smaller grain; that known as No. 2 basket powder has frequently been found to give the best all-round results in these small bores. The moral of all this is, leave the very large grain powders for the rifles they were originally intended for. Here, their slow combustion and less recoil are advantages that can hardly be over-rated.

Another immense improvement in the manufacture of black powder during the last few years has been the introduction of great compression of the "meal" by hydraulic press, whereby a pressure equal to some sixty-five to seventy tons to the square foot is placed upon it, of course greatly increasing its density, which not only effects its rapidity of ignition, but also, being so much harder, it takes a better and cleaner glazing, and, so to speak, wears better, that is, it is not so liable to rub into dust in transit, &c. And this matter of density, too, is a material factor in the velocity imparted to the charge.

There has been an almost universal feeling that sporting black powder deteriorates considerably by keeping, and certainly the writer's own experience goes to confirm this, as he almost invariably found that black powder kept over from one season to the next had materially gone off in strength. But it must be borne in mind that experiments to this end, conducted with any ordinary "powder tryer," can never be at all reliable – the conditions can never be equal either as to the machine itself or atmospherically. What has confirmed the belief has been that the new issues of the same brand from the same firm are generally, if tried against the old, considerably the stronger; but I am not prepared to say that this falling off in power in the one season would be very appreciable in the field, though I fancy it would be so at the plate. However, at this moment, no experiments can be turned up which would tend to elucidate this point; though it is a fact that, at the field trials of explosives in 1878, Mr. Pigou, one of the present partners in that eminent firm, brought down with him one day at the end of the trial some powder of the firm's make, *known* to be nearly ninety years old. The writer was requested to try this powder, which was done out of an excellent modified choke. What this powder may have been originally it is, of course, impossible to say, but this is certain, that better powder than it was then need not be wished for. The result of every shot was excellent in both pattern and penetration, and the recoil, considering the fine grain, very moderate. This powder was of extraordinarily fine grain and very even, an excellent colour, very hard, and was perfectly clean – in fact, not a fault could be found with it, and its trial was most interesting, and certainly went to prove that the deterioration in this case, if any, must have been exceedingly small.

As regards our own great makers – which really means the great makers of the world – viz., Messrs. Curtis and Harvey, Pigou and Co., and Hall and Sons, no appreciable difference can be found in their best sporting powders. They are *all* so excellent that a man using black powder cannot do wrong in his choice, provided he chooses a moderate-sized grain as before stated – say, not larger than No. 4 or 5 at most.

Of any foreign productions little need be said. Happily for the writer, few have come under his notice, but those few have been the most wretchedly miserable compounds that could well be imagined, being small grained, dirty, soft, and dusty in the extreme, filthy in use, and fouling the guns to a degree that could hardly be credited by those used to our own English make; and, still worse, some of them appear to be almost as "quick" as gun-cotton, thereby greatly, perhaps alarmingly, increasing the strain on the barrels, besides, of course, giving bad and irregular shooting.

The above allusion to gun-cotton reminds one of the craze this stuff created some five-and-thirty years or so ago, when the first question of almost every shooting friend you met was "Have you seen this wonderful new gun-cotton? Have you tried it?" Ten to one, a small quantity was produced from some mysterious little box or other, and you were invited to try the experiment of having a small piece ignited in your hand. Nay! Even young ladies would cheerfully submit their delicate pretty little white palms to the process, and point to the fact of their not being even soiled, or the delicate whiteness sullied by it. Well, it was a very pretty toy for such pleasant and innocent amusements; but for sporting purposes utterly useless, and worse – absolutely dangerous. The write was, however, induced (against his own judgment), at the request of some shooting friends, to experiment with it, and for this purpose application was made to the Messrs. Hall (who had then lately bought Schonbien's patent), who not only most handsomely provided a considerable quantity of the article, but also gave the formula for its manufacture at home, but the results were so singularly and utterly erratic that nothing could possibly be done with it. One end of a small batch, manipulated with the greatest care throughout the whole process, would come out with an energy so uncontrollable as to endanger the safety of the gun if nothing worse, while the other end, with a similar load, would not drive the shot many yards from the muzzle, and certainly would not have hurt a pound of butter at thirty. About this time, too, the late Mr. Charles Lancaster burst a gun, happily without ill consequences, with it; though how a man of his practical knowledge and experience could have ventured on a load of seventy-five grains – which he himself told the writer was the bursting charge – was always a mystery. It has always been a source of congratulation to the writer that he himself came out of those experiments with a proper and normal complement of extremities!

None of the other modern nitro compounds need be touched upon in a paper like this – confined entirely to sporting purposes as they are, and probably ever will be. All are far too rapid and dangerously energetic to be ever even thought of in a shot gun, save and except the one great and crowning invention in explosives for the sportsman, namely, the Schultze wood powder. There can be but little doubt that, at no very distant date, this is destined to be *the* sportsman's powder of the future.

When this powder was first brought over here (about 1868 or 1869) one of the leading West End gunmakers requested the writer to give it a trial and report the results to him. This was some time prior to the formation of any company for its manufacture here. It was seen at once that any small trial of a few guns could not be satisfactory; the writer therefore put himself in communication with a gunmaker in his neighbourhood, who, on having the circumstances explained to him, at once most handsomely placed the whole of his stock at the writer's disposal. This enabled him to set to work with a will, and the trial was conducted in this way:- Each gun was first tried with various loads of black powder, so as to find its best shooting. Then the gun was cleaned and alternate shots were taken with black and its equivalent in comparison of the two powders being always carried out from first to last on the same day. If the weather prevented this it was started again. This trial altogether occupied (with pretty constant shooting) over three months, and comprised some thousands of shots out of from fifty to sixty guns, from the highest priced and best finished weapons of the crack London makers down to the cheapest Birmingham guns, and the result was that out of all these there was but one that did not give much harder and better shooting with wood than with black; and this one notable exception, though by no means one of the cheapest guns, was so irretrievably bad that nothing could be made of it with any load of either powder. This trial was so exhaustive and eminently satisfactory to the writer that from this time to the present he has exclusively used the wood powder, and never fired a single shot of black, except in experimental trial shooting at the target, and for the purposes of comparison.

It came out originally in the form of a "cube" powder, though never the shape of "sawdust," as it was then often ironically termed – in fact, the writer was known among his shooting friends for several years by that cognomen in consequence of his steady adherence to and advocacy of this powder. And it was remarked by one of the leading manufacturers of the black; "Ah! I don't care what may be said about this sawdust or who takes it up, it will never do us any harm. They *can never granulate* it, and until they do it will be worth nothing." What would he had said now? As we have for years had it in this shape, and it is in every way admirable.

That it will ever do the manufacturers of black any serious injury is unlikely, as not being adapted to either rifles (save the very small bores) or artillery, that monopoly (the principal part of their trade) must remain with them; but that it will eventually, if it does not at present, materially affect the sale of their sporting powders there can be no question.

The advantages of this most excellent explosive are so obvious and well-known that it would almost seem unnecessary to refer to them here. Still perhaps it would be better to notice some of them. First and foremost then, almost ninety-nine out of every hundred guns will shoot better and closer with it. The recoil is greatly less than with its equivalent in black, and the smoke is not only not a third of what is given off by black, but what there is is so thin and transparent as to be readily seen through; so much so, that the writer, in all the years he has used this powder, cannot recall a *single* instance in which he has been prevented by smoke from putting in his second barrel, and a gun fouls so little with it that hundreds of shots may be fired without requiring wiping out. A slight tap with the fingers on the barrels while the gun is open, causes nearly the whole of the residuum to fall out; and las, but not least, you may shoot for a month without soiling your hands, nor are you ever annoyed with the disagreeable smell arising from the sulphur in the other. And it is a remarkable fact that the products of the combustion of this powder are entirely *alkaline*, so that the acids wearing out the guns, that we even still sometimes hear of, is simply a "myth." The truth of the above statement can be verified by anyone who will take the trouble to wash out a gun after using wood powder and try the water with a piece of litmus test paper; in fact, it can be freely asserted that a gun is never known to get a single speck of rust arising from its use *per se*.

Another, not a small advantage, is that it has no affinity for damp, and really scarcely ever requires drying, as, if slightly damped, it shoots as well and "goes" as quickly as ever. This was proved by the writer, who subjected a small quantity of it to a process of steaming until its density was considerably increased, and immediately loading some shells, and taking them out for trial at the place, where no difference could be seen between them and the dry powder, used for comparison. Should, however, drying be really considered necessary, some care should be taken in the process, as it must not be subjected to too great a heat. The best plan is to place a few plates in boiling water till hot through, wipe them perfectly dry, and scatter the powder over them, not more than half an inch thick. This will do all that is required, and the powder had better be left on the plates to cool in a dry room until the *next* day. At any rate, be careful to avoid loading it or using it in a hot state, as if the temperature is raised beyond a certain point, the energy of the powder appears to be greatly increased. It is thought the drying of *loaded* cartridges should, if possible, be avoided, but if absolutely necessary don't *overdo* it. Put them away for three or four days, and stand them up singly in a cool dry room before use to ensure their thoroughly cooling through. To shew how little all this is really necessary, the writer has never *once,* after a use of twelve or thirteen years (during which no more than common and ordinary care has been taken), found it necessary to dry a *single* cartridge or a charge of the powder!

There is another point also worth the consideration of sportsmen, especially those going abroad, and that is that this powder does not suffer in the smallest degree by keeping any length of time. A few months ago the writer would have said that, on the contrary, it was certainly benefited by it; but he can hardly do this in the face of the careful experiments – lately carried out by Mr. Charles Rosson, of Derby, at a "field force gauge," with wood powders – of the last four years, issued and published in the *Field*; whereby it appeared that the powder of 1881 really shot somewhat the steadiest of all, but the difference between the oldest and most recent was so trifling as to thoroughly prove the truth of the first position. Moreover, the writer has now in his possession some of the first sample of Schultze he ever possessed, which in a trial not very long ago, with the same load and from the same gun as it was originally tried with, gave within a very small fraction the same results from a similar number of shots, shewing satisfactorily that neither powder nor gun had deteriorated, as the small difference could be fully accounted for atmospherically.

A great deal has been said and written about the difficulty of loading with this powder. The writer himself has done so, but has been partially misunderstood. If anyone asserts that wood powder requires great care in loading he will agree with him at once, but will say immediately, "And so does black." Take what powder you will, if the shells are carelessly or improperly loaded good results can *never* be expected; and a man who always carefully loads his own cartridges will always enjoy his sport the more, as he will shoot with perfect confidence, and know to a nicety what his gun will do and what to expect from it. It is quite certain that precisely the same materials in every respect may be put into half a given number of cases by a man who knows how to load and the other half by one who is simply told or shewn how to do it, and the results at the plate will probably vary by from 15 to 20 per cent. Depend on it, care and experience, and knowledge too, *must* be applied to loading – whatever powder is used – if good and *regular* results are to be expected; and it must not be forgotten that a *single* carelessly or improperly loaded cartridge in a match may lose a man a cup or a pool.

So much has been said in favour of wood powder that the writer thinks he had better add that he is *not* a shareholder in the company, nor has he the remotest interest in it, in any way. What he has written has been in the interests of shooters, from the firm conviction of the thorough goodness of the article, derived from constant use for many years in field and covert, and many thousands of shots at the plate.

One who has Fired some 20,000 Trial Shots at Marks.

From *THE SPORTING MIRROR,* May 1882.

IN THE ARTICLE entitled "Modern Gunpowders," published in the SPORTING MIRROR for April, our correspondent, "One who has Fired some 20,000 Trial Shots at Marks," in reference to the diamond grain gunpowder remarks, "If recollection serves, the first innovation of the diamond grain was by the Messrs. Hall, and a great improvement it was." Messrs. Curtis and Harvey write and inform us that this is an error on the part of the writer, as they introduced the grain, it being their own specialite (sic), and has been made solely by them since its introduction over forty years ago. [We deeply regret that this unfortunate mistake should have occurred, and hasten to make every reparation in our power.] – ED. S.M.

A.J. Lane on Cartridge Loading

With *The Sporting Mirror* article titled "How to Load a Gun", we are at the very core of Arthur Lane's convictions that quality ammunition was essential for good shooting and that loads needed to be tailored to specific guns. The fact that, today, the overwhelming majority of those who use a shotgun have no idea how their guns shoot is surprising, given that there is a wide ranging corps of folklore on the vagaries of shotguns. This apathy in no way compromises the truth of A.J.L.'s beliefs.

As an insight into the forces which lead Arthur Lane to load all his own cartridges, we have his letter to *The Field* of November 21st 1881.

> Now most of the cartridges you buy are often loaded all sorts of ways; the loads especially of powder are usually very unequal, varying even a quarter of a drachm. The waddings are put in in all sorts of ways, and with widely different force, and generally are too slack to insure easy loading of the shells; and the shot is not always regular or what it is marked. I do not wish or intend to bring a charge against the many highly respectable and conscientious gunmakers who take great pains in the loading; but the faults are, I think inherent in the Erskine machine, by which they are loaded by the thousand by lads and girls, who know as much of guns and shooting as an elephant. I have frequently found wadding put in at a considerable angle from using too small a rammer; and not long ago I discovered a thick wad actually edgeways, so that at the sides there was nothing between powder and shot and they

both partly ran out together on removing the top wad. Only last season, requiring shot at a friend's for the last day, I sent to the neighbouring town for a few loaded cartridges. I could do nothing with them. On examining the few remaining on my return home, I found the powder to be fair, but fine grain, no two were alike in quantity but all ¼ dr or less than the specified load; one miserable soft wad over the powder and shot which purported to be No 5 was mixed 5 & 6, with a fair sprinkling of 4s amongst them, with one exception of one which contained an honest charge of No 6. The top wads (in sight) were good cloth wads.

What is perhaps remarkable about his essay is that there is virtually no discussion on the choice of components, it is simply assumed that hard shot, felt wadding and Schultze powder will be used. Perhaps the constraints of space dictated this approach, so to give a more rounded account, it might be of value if we look at A.J.L.'s writings on these points, which appeared as letters to *The Field*.

On the subject of wadding, the following informative letter appeared a decade later, but it is relevant at this point. In today's parlance, the white wool felt described as "25W – i.e. 0.25G/cc cubed" conforms to Lane's description and, in the author's experience, produces excellent wads.

SOFT FELT WADS

SIR – Your correspondent "No 5" is perfectly right in all he says regarding hard and rigid wads; but he might have said three or four times as much and yet been within the truth. I have had almost endless experiments in loading and I believe nearly all the wadding that I have ever been brought out, but with these hard wadding, the results were always such that for many years I have not allowed them to enter my gun room. There is no doubt but a great number of loaded cartridges supplied to unsuspecting sportsmen will be found to contain them; and I am certain they are quite enough to mar the even and regular shooting of the best guns that can be made. Moreover if they are a tight fit in the shell and fired from a choke gun they increase the strain on the barrel to an extent many sportsmen have little idea of, as well as unpleasantly augmenting the recoil.

In reply to his question as to where really good soft and pliable felt wads can be obtained the best I have ever seen or used came from Mr W Ford, gunmaker, Eclipse Works, Loveday Street, Birmingham. He supplies them in all thickness form I believe 1/8in. up to 5/8in.; but I have generally found that for general shooting the 1/2in. wads are the best. I must warn "No 5" however that with these soft wads the tier of shot next them at times gets so firmly bedded in the soft felt that they do not altogether leave it for a long way from the gun, in which case the wad is not infrequently from the greatly increased weight carried up to the place at 40 yards; but this is entirely obviated if the formula I have used for a great many years by followed – that is always put a dry thin card wad wadding between the shot and the thick wad.

THE FIELD, August 6th 1892 (Page 241)

By today's thinking, it is odd that there is no mention of matching the primer to the powder, because again there are no contemporary references to different types of caps, as they were then called. These were to emerge a decade or more later.

By contrast, the powder to be used was a matter of great importance, because the only explanation of contemporary accounts is that, in some establishments, quality control was far below what, today, is taken for granted. Arthur Lane was a lifelong advocate of Schultze.

Schultze

Running through the writings of Arthur Lane, there are many references to Schultze propellant powder. Now long off the market, it is relevant to Lane's story that some account concerning this product be included.

The name is that of its inventor, Capt. Johannes Eduard Schultze, a Prussian artillery officer. In essence, this propellant is created by the action of strong nitric acid on wood and was one of a group of highly reactive compounds that had first been prepared in the first half of the 19th century by the action of nitric acid on a wide range of organic materials.

The properties, and hence the usefulness, of these products varied in part with the substrate, but also with the way the treatment was undertaken and the subsequent modifying procedures. So while there were several processes that refined the characteristics of Schultze, it was residual microstructures of the wood that was of value in defining its performance.

Part of the significance of Schultze derives from the fact that it was the first commercially successful substitute for black gunpowder that was marketed in Great Britain. Thus it became the yardstick by which later offerings were judged and, in turn, it was modified to remain competitive with the said later arrivals.

A company was formed in Great Britain in 1868 to exploit its commercial potential. The market for the product was a diverse collection of users, gunmakers who loaded on varying scales for their customers and individuals who loaded for their own use. Faced with this mix of customers, the company made the wise decision that their product had to be compatible with not just the guns but also the cartridge cases, caps (primers) and wadding then in use. It also had to occupy the same volume, load for load, as black powder.

That the company was successful in its pursuit of these goals, we can judge in part from the praise that Arthur Lane bestowed, which, in turn, can only have enhanced Schultze's reputation.

In this context, it is perhaps surprising that there was so little mention in Lane's writings of the evolution of the product. It may be that he was not aware of the changes which, at the time, would have been commercial secrets. What is certain is that in 1878 the product altered form when it was granulated. Then, in 1885, it was waterproofed and finally, in 1894, the grains were hardened.

Perhaps the explanation of Lane's lack of comment on these changes is that they were all intended to make the powder less susceptible to misuse and so of little relevance to a loader as careful as he.

While there was never, to my knowledge, a complete recipe of how to make Schultze published, in later years, when they were of merely historical interest, more facts did emerge.

For instance, in the obituary of the chief chemist, and in large part the architect of the success of Schultze, W.S. Griffith (published in *Arms & Explosives* of April 1906), we find an account of the species and forms of the wood used as a substrate. These were variously, alder, pine and finally white poplar in 1877, which was used for the rest of the commercial life of the product. Given the quantities involved, questions are raised as to the source of this timber and the possibility that it was grown specially.

Not only did the wood used vary with time, mention is also made variously of the form of the wood. Originally the product was wood fibres, then crumbs formed by cutting a thin slice or veneer off the end-grain and crumbling the result. The pine was actual sawdust and, finally, the poplar was pulped and granules created from this.

Like so much of this story, these are but the broad outlines and it is obvious that fine technical details are missing, perhaps now lost forever.

As always, we are left with more questions than answers.

SCHULTZE GUNPOWDER

TRADE MARK.

Highest Honours wherever Exhibited.

LONDON	...	1885	CALIFORNIA	...	1894	MILAN	...	1894
CHICAGO	...	1893	ANTWERP	...	1894	ATLANTA	...	1895
		BRUSSELS	...	...	...	1897.		

"SCHULTZE" THE ORIGINAL SMOKELESS POWDER.

PIGEON SHOOTING.

All Principal Events at Home and Abroad have been won with SCHULTZE POWDER.

The Amateur Championship of America	1895
The Professional Championship of America	1895
The Championship at Spa	1895
The Championship at Aix-les-Bains	1895
The Championship at Bosnia	1896
The Champion Stakes (Hurlingham)	1896
The Champion Stakes (Gun Club) Divided	1896
The Amateur Championship of America	1897
The Challenge Cup, Melbourne	1897
The Gun Club Challenge Cup won outright	1897
The Triennial Championship (Monte Carlo) ... ...1889 to	1898
The Grand Prix du Casino (Monte Carlo)	1898
The Grand Prix du Cloture (Monte Carlo)	1898
The Grand American Handicap, 197 Competitors	1898
The Gun Club £100 Challenge Cup won outright	1898
The Belgium £100 Cup (International Meeting)	1898
The Gun Club £200 International Cup	1898
The Grande Poule D'Essai (Monte Carlo), 103 Competitors ...	1899
The Prix D'Ouverture (Monte Carlo), 117 Competitors	1899
The Gun Club International Cup	1900
The Members' Challenge Cup (International Meeting)	1900
The 32 yards Sweepstakes	1900

SUPPLIED IN CANISTERS AND CARTRIDGES.

WHOLESALE ONLY—

THE SCHULTZE GUNPOWDER Co., Ltd.
28, GRESHAM STREET, LONDON, E.C.

Experimental and Specialised Cartridges

The Sporting Mirror article describes what might be termed ordinary cartridges. Inevitably, Arthur Lane experimented further. Thus we have accounts of him producing both spreader and long-range cartridges.

Details of five loads for spreader cartridges were published in *The Field* of November 17th 1888, Volume 72.

> NO. 1 – 3drs black or 42grs Schultze, one card grease proof, two pink edge wads, 1 1/8oz shot, one pink edge, this slightly spreads the charge.
>
> NO. 2 – same powder, one card grease proof, one pink edge, same shot, two pink edge wads, gives a wider spread.
>
> NO. 3 – same powder, one stout grease proof card, same shot, two pink edge wads, this usually will give a spread of nearly 4feet but does not shoot as strong as the former.
>
> NO. 4 – same loading as No 1 but divide the shot in half with a card wad. This gives a broad spread without interfering materially with the strength. A still wider spread by dividing the shot with thin card wadding into three equal portions instead of two.
>
> NO. 5 – 45grs of Schultze, one card, one pink edge, 1oz of No 5, two pink edge on top. This in most guns is a most deadly load up to 40 yards and gives a fair spread, and is the one I generally adopt. Some of the other loadings give a much broader circle but I consider this enough for any fair shot.

The recipe for long-range ammunition appeared in *The Field* of March 20th 1880.

> Use the ordinary load of Schultze, or four or five grains extra are added as above, and 3/4oz of No 4, put in a few shot and well shake down amongst it a little well baked or otherwise thoroughly dried beech or other hardwood sawdust, repeat the operation until the whole charge is put in and a little dust on top; wad with a slack thin card turned over just enough to hold. Loaded in this way my 16 bore Greener puts nearly the whole charge, 120 pellets in the 30inch circle at fifty yards, seldom more than five or ten outside and these quite close.
>
> The reduced load of large shot (my general load being 1oz) gives a high velocity and the sawdust tends to keep the shot together.

Finally, there is an experiment which was, frankly, dangerous – a modification of the cartridge cap. In *The Field* of January 14th 1882, Volume 59, on page 58 we read:

> In experimenting when the charge of the cap was increased by one half (which was done by scraping the powder from caps, carefully weighing and replacing with a touch of lac varnish to secure it) in almost every case the shot was more or less wild with great irregularity of pattern and a palpably increased recoil.

The danger in this is twofold. On the one hand cap compositions are, by their very nature, sensitive mixtures and not suitable to be disturbed. Even worse on the other hand, the effects of using these modified caps sounds like increased breech pressure caused by a more rapid combustion of the propellant charge.

Please do not try this at home!

"The Rivière and Baker machines are far away the best I have ever tried."

THE FIELD, 2nd half 1881 (Page 355)

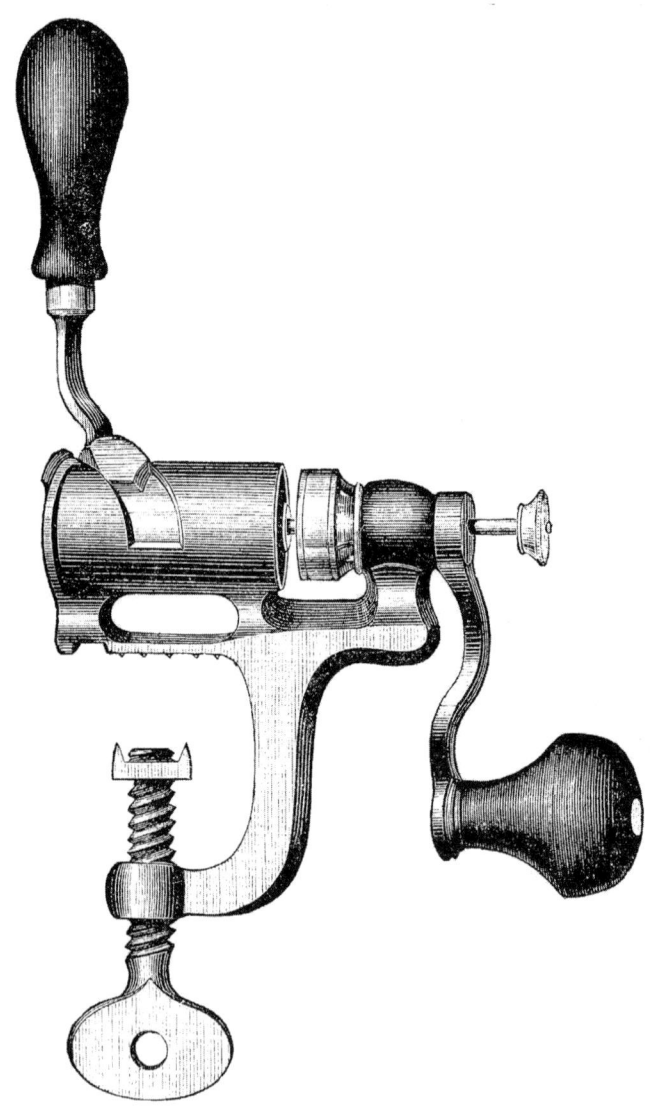

Henry Rivière & Thomas Baker, patent No. 1865 of 1868

Jones' Wad Press

To the best of my knowledge, there are only four references to the W.P. Jones wad press in the sporting literature of the 19th century. These are the application for a patent*, an advertorial in *The Field*, a listing in a C.G. Bonehill catalogue and A.J.L.'s instructions for the use of this device, again in *The Field*. Moreover, there is no known surviving example of this tool.

Taken together, these facts suggest that the device was a commercial failure and that there were not enough cartridge loaders prepared to go to the trouble of using such a tool.

No doubt the price – £6 in the Bonehill catalogue – was also a deterrent. This seems very expensive as a very serviceable if plain double barrel gun could have been purchased for the same amount.

Despite all this, from our present perspective, Lane's account is of value, not least as an insight into the care with which he loaded his ammunition.

>……..With long experience I think I can give G.G. a hint or two worth having, in the first place carefully measure and then weigh one charge; put this into the shell, tap on the table to shake it down close and even, then I take one of Mr Jones's most admirable loaders, screw in the head proper for the size of the shell; this will just drop easily in. When this rests on the powder, set the disc to the level of the top of the shell, slightly nip it to prevent its shifting, take it out, place the left thumbnail under it on the graduated side of the loader, then shift the disc till it is 1/16in above the thumbnail

and nip it up tight, then press the loader on to every charge of powder as far as it will go. This pressure I have found suitable for all gauges.

While *The Field* advertorial and the Bonehill catalogue are illustrated – both probably from the same block owned by the inventor – the renditions are of poor quality. This drawing is an enhanced tracing produced by the author.

A.J.L. also mentions use of the Jones 'Accuratus' powder measure.

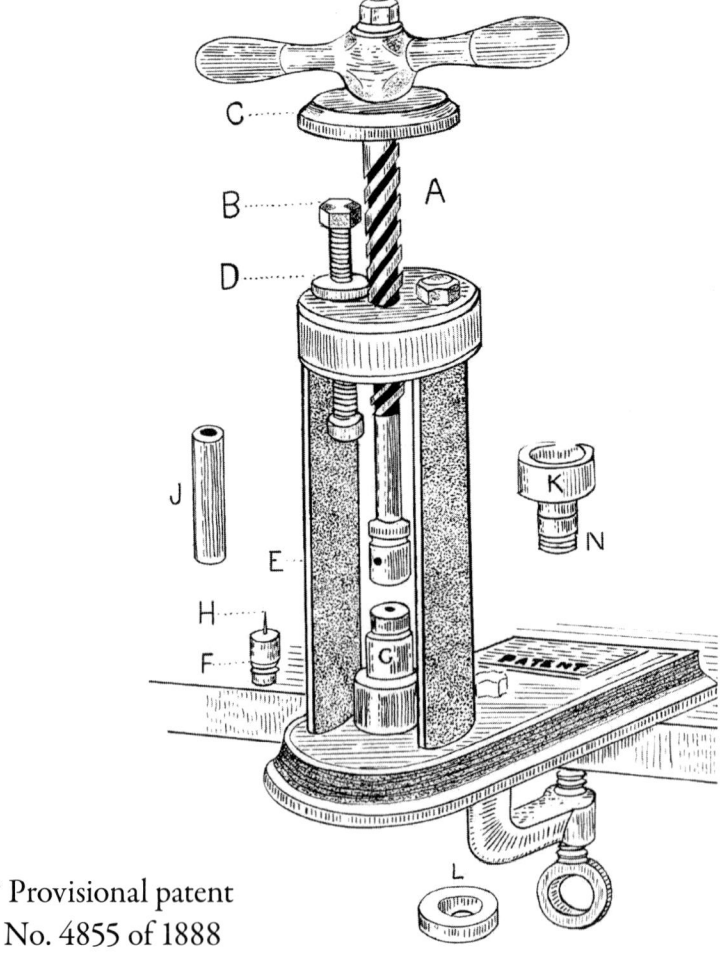

* Provisional patent No. 4855 of 1888

How to Load a Gun

Despite its title, the very narrow approach of this piece, which would severely limit its contemporary usefulness, conversely makes it of value for this study, because it could have more accurately have been called "How I Load Cartridges and some Experiences at the Pattern Plate". So, in essence, we have more shooting autobiography, which adds to our knowledge of A.J. Lane.

In the one hundred and thirty odd years that have passed since it was written, some of the components listed have become obsolete. Today it would be difficult to find 'Wood Powder' (otherwise Schultze), or 'Pink Edge' wads which were cut from thin sheets of dense felt – one side grease-proofed with a black compound, the other lubricated with a substance containing a red dye. The exact nature of the grease-proofer or the lubricant seem never to have been published.

Even if they could be found, the vagaries of the inevitable long storage only add more weight to the disclaimer that the table of loads is quoted for historical interest only and not as recommendations for practical use.

Unsurprisingly, Arthur wrote several essays on this subject, in particular a long letter to *The Field*, which John H. Walsh reproduced in Volume I of *The Modern Sportsman's Gun & Rifle* - a further illustration of the ties between these two pundits.

HOW TO LOAD A GUN

HAVING IN A recent paper considered the leading points for consideration in the choice of a gun, the next subject that presents itself is how to load it so as to get the best possible results out of it. It need hardly be said that the finest gun in the world sinks into simple mediocrity unless served with charges calculated to develop its powers. And it must be premised that cylinders and soft shot are considered behind the age, and therefore in this paper it must be understood chokes and hard shot are alone referred to.

It may be stated to start with that nearly all gunmakers of the present day bore their guns for, and regulate them to, certain charges, at forty yards range, and for No. 6 shot, which are usually these: $3\frac{1}{4}$drms. and $1\frac{1}{8}$oz. for a 12-bore; $2\frac{3}{4}$drms. and 1oz. for a 16-bore; and $2\frac{1}{2}$drms. and $1\frac{1}{8}$oz.* for a 20-bore, and of these bores only it is proposed to treat in this paper. Someone may very likely say, that being the case, why need the sportsman trouble himself further; let him accept his gunmaker's load and report, buy his cartridges of him ready loaded, and "rest and be thankful." True; and this *may* do for a good many shooters, but will never satisfy a genuine scientific sportsman, as he well knows that when for different game the range varies, or a change in the size of shot becomes necessary, there is not one gun in a thousand that will not make far better shooting by not only varying the weights of either powder and shot, or both, but also the number, thickness, and distribution of the wadding used.

Another point is worth consideration; the actual trial of guns is a matter attended with so much expense, and occupies so much time with the makers, that they cannot afford to try what may be called extra experiments; they try their guns with what may be called regulation loads, and when they reach their standard they are finished

---

*It is very likely that $\frac{7}{8}$oz is the intending weight here [Ed].

and sent to their customers; they try nothing further, nor are they (for the reasons above) to be blamed in this respect. But it by no means follows that nothing better is to be got aby a further adjustment of the load. In proof of this I may state that I now possess a 16-bore by one of the best London makers, which is equivalent to saying one of the best in the world. The load sent me with the gun was 2½drms. by measure, wood powder, and 1oz. No. 6. On trial the shooting was excellent, quite up to the report made to me by the maker, but there were certain indications in the distribution of the pellets, the size and shape of the marks on the plate, &c., almost impossible to describe, but still palpable to an experienced eye, which induced me to think that more powder would improve the shooting. I consequently tried 2¾drms. The pattern was thinner, but harder. I then tried 3drms. (a maximum load for a 16-bore), still with the same wads and 1oz. No. 6; the result was a closer pattern, much more even, nearly every pellet standing out singly and very much harder. The average is 150 in a 24-inch circle. This would be hard to beat! Yet these barrels are but twenty-two inches long, and the gun weighs but 5lb. 7oz. In the face of such facts it is idle to say short guns will not shoot or will not burn a large charge of powder.

It may be taken for granted that all guns will do best if kept strictly to the sized shot for which they have been regulated; but, when a change becomes necessary, in most cases they will do relatively better if the next sizes are missed, - that is, if a gun has been bored for No. 6, it will most likely shoot better with No. 4 or 8 than with 5 or 7. By the term relatively, I mean with reference to the number of pellets contained in the charge, and that put into the 30-inch circle; and, to my fancy, to make the most of a 12-bore it should always be regulated to shoot No. 5 in preference to a smaller size. The gun is just as good for close quarters, and is infinitely superior at fifty or sixty yards, and in these long ranges lies the only advantage of the wide bore, unless indeed a man is so bad a shot as to wish a pattern that covers a barn door at forty yards, in which case a 12-bore cylinder will suit him best. No. 6 is most suitable for a 16-bore, and a 20 may be regulated for either No. 6 or 7, according to the fancy of the owner. For myself I should prefer the larger size, as with it a full-choked 20 can be made to put on a very killing pattern up to fifty yards, or perhaps a little over, but they are of course, in consequence of the smaller load, far behind a 12 at sixty.

On the trial of a gun the first thing to find out is the *largest* charge of powder it will burn when properly wadded behind the normal load of No. 6 shot for the bore as stated above. This is readily found by a few shots with increasing loads. A practised eye will at once detect the increased force from the mark (of the lead, not the splash) on the plate, and probably after a few increases in the weight of powder the force will be found to actually *diminish*. This at once shews that more powder is put in than the barrel will burn; that it is, in fact, blown out unignited and only fired *after* it has left the muzzle. M Return at once to the load that gave the greatest force with the least powder, and *never* vary this as long as you use the same sized shot. Now try the effect of a little more or a little less weight of shot, and it will be readily seen which makes the best pattern. And here let me warn the young sportsman or the tyro at plate trials that it is often not the load that puts the most pellets on to the 30-inch circle that is the best, but that which gives the most even distribution over the plate, with the pellets standing out pretty much singly, not bunched up in fours and fives, with spaces between where a "bird" or a snipe might escape, and that giving the greatest equality, that is, shewing the least variation between the highest and lowest number put on in a series of shots. And this constitutes the really good, reliable, killing gun.

The next point for consideration is when a change in the size of shot becomes necessary or desirable. Having ascertained the exact load of No. 6 by the means above pointed out, supposing the gun to be a 12-bore, about one-eighth of an ounce may be added for each increase in the size, and a similar reduction should be made when using the smaller sizes; thus, if the load of No. 6 is 1⅛., for No. 5 it may be 1¼oz., for No. 4 1⅜oz; the other way, if No. 7 is used, 1oz., or if No. 8, ⅞. will be enough. The "rationale" of this is simply that the larger the shot the less is the friction and resistance in the barrel; hence the loads may be increased in weight as above stated without appreciably adding to the labour or recoil so as to make the used of the gun unpleasant, and for the same reason reversed, the loads of the smaller sizes are reduced.

It will generally be found that in using No. 4, or larger shot, much better patterns will be got by reducing the powder by about a quarter of a dram or so, and the force will be still quite sufficient in consequence of the greatly increased momentum of the large shot; whereas, on the other hand, in using No. 8 it is better to increase the load of powder a quarter to three-eighths of a dram; the force will be increased and the pattern will be better distributed and more killing. And it must always be kept in mind that at long ranges with the larger sizes of shot a larger proportion of the whole charge will be put on the circle than with smaller shot. For instance, I have a 12-bore that will put on more No. 5's at sixty yards than it will No. 6, though there are many more pellets in the charge of No. 6 than there are in the charge of No. 5. For a 16-bore the increase in weight beyond the ascertained load of No. 6 for each size will be about **three thirty seconds** oz. and for a 20-bore **one sixteenth**, and the reductions for smaller shot will be in these proportions with both gauges.

I must here warn all young sportsmen that in the shooting of a gun positively *nothing* must be taken for granted. No two guns ever shoot exactly alike; even the same gun will not give the same results or averages on two different days. Though they may be often approximately near, at another trial there may be a wide and unaccountable divergence, and, in loading, what is sauce for the goose is often by no means sauce for the gander. A load altered according to the above suggestions may answer exceedingly well out of one gun, but may not do at all out of another of the same bore, &c., and such is the fickleness and uncertainty of guns generally that I would impress on everyone who delights in and wishes to get all he can out of a gun that *no load whatever* should be used in the field until it has been thoroughly tried and worked out at the target.

It will frequently be found that when the increased weight of large shot is used that larger charges of powder *can* be burnt behind it; this arises from the greater force that is required to start the shot in the barrel, which gives more time for the ejection of the powder before the charge leaves the muzzle of the gun. This is useful in large and strong and heavy flock guns, as it gives a greater velocity and a wider spread to the pellets, but is not desirable in ordinary game guns, as it enormously increases the strain on both barrels and action, produces a heavy recoil and tends to the loosening of the "joint" and rapid wearing-out of the gun. Still there are times at which an extra hardness in the shooting *may* be specially wanted; it is therefore well to know that it can be got; but it is better avoided, as I have known the shooting of guns much impaired, besides other injuries arising from it, and should, I think, not be ventured on unless the gun is a "cross bolt" action.

It must be borne in mind that the whole of the above suggestions are not given as *rules*, as *no* hard and fast rules *can* be laid down, but simply as shewing the general principles of the science of loading (for a science it truly is), and to enable a young shooter or a beginner in experimental target-shooting to start with fair prospect of arriving at what he wants.

The subject of wadding now demands our attention, and it is so great a factor in the shooting of a gun that some little consideration must be bestowed upon it. For my own part I employ and thoroughly recommend the use of four kinds.

1st. – A grease-proof one to be placed next the powder. This should be a *tight* fit in the shell, and must be thoroughly greased and fire proof. I like none so well as the thin brown varnished card wads made by Kynoch and Co. These answer *all* the required conditions, and there is *no* lamp-black in the varnish to burn off and increase the fouling left in the barrel.

2nd. – A pink edge wad to go on the grease-proof. This should also be a tight fit.

3rd. – A thick felt wad. This should not fit so tight, and should be a solid, firm wad, by no means hard, but easily compressible by the thumb and fingers.

4th. – A thin card wad to go on the thick felt. This should be quite an easy (or slack) fit, and the same wad should be used over the shot, as to get the best shooting the less there is put over the shot the better, provided it is just enough when the case is turned down to prevent the charge shaking loose on firing the first barrel.

It will be observed this is the mode of wadding when the hardest and closest, in fact the best, shooting is desired. When it is wished to spread the charge for closer quarters use only Nos. 1 and 2 wads on the powder, and one or two No. 2 on the shot. For still closer work (twenty to twenty-five yards) use Nos. 1 and 2 on the powder as before, and divide the charge of shot into three equal portions with a card wad No. 4 between each and one or two No. 2 wads on the top of the shot. If a still wider spread is wished the load of shot may be reduced. But it is not desirable to reduce the charge of powder as suggested by some writers. The mere alterations in the mode of wadding already materially affect the strength of the shooting, and it is not well to reduce it yet more by using a smaller weight of powder unless a larger-sized shot is used, in which case the greater weight of the individual pellets will pretty well balance the weaker discharge of a smaller load of powder. But it must not be forgotten the larger the size of the shot employed, the *smaller* will be the disc covered at any given distance in all cases.

It now, I think, but remains to say a few words on the actual *modus operandi* of loading the shells, and I most emphatically advise every shooter to do this for himself, as when bought ready loaded they are mostly those supplied to the gunmakers by those who load in bulk and are by them retailed to their customers. These are loaded with an Erskine or some such machine, and little reliance can, I fear, in most cases, by placed in either quantities or qualities of the contents, and are almost invariably badly or improperly wadded and rammed, an inherent fault of the machine. If they *must* be bought loaded, go to some maker known to you and who loads himself for his customers, or employs really qualified hands for the work, and do not entrust your sport to the manipulations of boys and girls who know as much about shooting and loading as a Cockney crossing-sweeper.

Nothing is said here of wire cartridges, concentrators, "et hoc genus omne." They are always useless out of a choke, and often absolutely dangerous in consequence of the fearfully increased strain thrown on the muzzle of the gun.

To return to loading. The first thing to be certain about is that the powder measures are correct. Thus 2½drms. should contain 35grs. of Schultze; the 2¾drms., 38½grs.; the 3drms., 42grs.; the 3¼drms., 45½grs.; and the 3½drms., 49grs.

The most convenient things to load from are deep and narrow china bowls (they are always dry and clean). Dip the measure, heaped up full, and give the handle two or three smart taps on the edge of the bowl, then strike off all remaining above the edges of the measure with the side of the empty shell, pour the powder into it, and, before setting it down, give it three or four smart taps on the table; this will settle the powder closely down, without leaving any spaces for air (more essential), and level at the top, without in any way wedging or caking it. Having thus filled all the shells, put in the card wad (No. 1), and just put it down with sufficient pressure to insure its resting firmly and evenly on the powder, but on no account to be rammed hard. N.B. – This wad may be omitted if the load is large, but I prefer to use it if there is room. If omitted, the pink edge should have a varnished grease-proof side to go next the powder; then put down a pink edge (No. 2), then the ordinary thick felt (No. 3), then a thin card (No.4). Some shooters and gunmakers think this last wadding unnecessary. I prefer it, for this reason, that I find in mark shooting, if omitted, the felt wads often fly right up to the plate at forty yards, at times even hit it, and are much impressed with the pattern of the shot lying next it, which probably cling therein for a considerable distance, and must greatly impede and interfere with the flight of these particular pellets, which ought to fly the hardest and straightest of the whole charge. Now, when the thin card wad (No. 4) is used under the shot, the thick felt wads stop many yards nearer the gun; and therefore I think it best used. The load of shot should be measured and stuck in the same manner as the powder; and on its use only a thin card (No. 4). About one tenth of an inch of the shell is enough to be left for turning down, and this should be turned down *firmly*. If more than 1⅛oz. of shot be used the pink edge (No. 2) wad may be omitted, as the increased resistance of the heavier load of shot appears to have nearly the same effect on the combustion; but in this case the card wadding (No. 1) should never be omitted.

There is a decided art in loading cartridges, and out of precisely the same materials some men will get much more than others; and this rests chiefly on the degree of pressure put on, but with a little practice and observation it is readily acquired. Of course care must be taken that there is not "shake" in any part of the load.

It will be seen that this plan of loading applies equally to black or wood powder, is what I always adopt, and is the experience of many years and many thousands of cartridges, as I invariably load with my own hands all shells intended for my own use.

The table of loads at the end of this paper will, I think, be found very useful for reference by those who may wish to go into this interesting matter practically, as I have suggested. But it must be fully understood that they are given *only* as landmarks and as guides, and as loads *likely* to produce good results; but, for the reasons before stated, it is impossible to say they *will* do so, but they may be safely trusted to use for commencing experiments with, to be varied after trial, as the appearance of pattern and force produced may dictate.

TABLE OF EXPERIMENTAL LOADS.

For a 12-Bore.

		About the No. of Pellets in charge and Newcastle chilled shot.
Powder, $2\frac{3}{4}$ drs.	Shot No. 3, $1\frac{1}{2}$ oz.	200
,, $2\frac{3}{4}$,,	,, ,, 4, $1\frac{3}{8}$,,	220
,, 3 ,,	,, ,, 5, $1\frac{1}{4}$,,	250
,, $3\frac{1}{4}$,,	,, ,, 6, $1\frac{1}{8}$,,	303
,, $3\frac{1}{4}$,,	,, ,, 7, 1 ,,	370
,, $3\frac{3}{8}$,,	,, ,, 8, $\frac{7}{8}$,,	417

For a 16-Bore.

Powder, $2\frac{1}{4}$ drs.	Shot No. 3, $1\frac{3}{16}$ oz	156
,, $2\frac{1}{2}$,,	,, ,, 4, $1\frac{1}{4}$,,	180
,, $2\frac{3}{4}$,,	,, ,, 5, $1\frac{1}{16}$,,	212
,, $2\frac{3}{4}$,,	,, ,, 6, 1 ,,	270
,, $2\frac{3}{4}$,,	,, ,, 7, $\frac{15}{16}$,,	347
,, 3 ,,	,, ,, 8, $\frac{7}{8}$,,	417

For a 20-Bore.

Powder, 2 drs.	Shot No. 3, $1\frac{1}{5}$ oz.	133
,, $2\frac{1}{4}$,,	,, ,, 4, $1\frac{1}{16}$,,	170
,, $2\frac{3}{8}$,,	,, ,, 5, 1 ,,	200
,, $2\frac{1}{2}$,,	,, ,, 6, $\frac{7}{8}$,,	237
,, $2\frac{1}{2}$,,	,, ,, 7, $\frac{3}{4}$,,	278
,, $2\frac{3}{4}$,,	,, ,, 8, $\frac{5}{8}$,,	300

N.B.—The last three loads of shot for this bore may often be advantageously increased to 1 oz., $\frac{7}{8}$ and $\frac{3}{4}$ respectively.

Table to shew about what may be expected on the *average from fairly good* shooting choke guns.

LOAD.	12-BORES.			Pattern 40 yards.	No. of sheets of Pettitt's pads penetrated.	Pattern 60 yards.	No. of sheets of Pettitt's pads penetrated.
$2\frac{3}{4}$ drs.	$1\frac{3}{8}$ oz.	No.	4	170	36	85	21
3 ,,	$1\frac{1}{4}$,,	,,	5	190	33	95	19
$3\frac{1}{4}$,,	$1\frac{1}{8}$,,	,,	6	210	29	100	16
$3\frac{3}{8}$,,	$\frac{7}{8}$,,	,,	8	240	19	105	10
	16-BORES.						
$2\frac{3}{4}$,,	$1\frac{1}{16}$,,	,,	5	165	32	75	19
$2\frac{3}{4}$,,	1 ,,	,,	6	180	28	85	16
$2\frac{3}{4}$,,	$\frac{15}{16}$,,	,,	7	200	24	90	14
3 ,,	$\frac{7}{8}$,,	,,	8	240	19	105	10
	20-BORES.						
$2\frac{3}{8}$,,	1 ,,	,,	5	120	30	60	18
$2\frac{1}{2}$,,	1 ,,	,,	6	175	26	85	13
$2\frac{1}{2}$,,	$\frac{7}{8}$,,	,,	7	190	23	90	11
$2\frac{3}{4}$,,	$\frac{3}{4}$,,	,,	8	205	19	92	10

N.B.—Really first-class "tip top" shooting guns will very considerably exceed the above figures.

One who has Fired 20,000 Shots at Marks.

The Kynoch 'Perfect' Cartridge Case

It is but another indication of A.J. Lane's standing in the shooting world that he should be one of the recipients of the promotional distribution of some of the early 'Perfects'. This new design of cartridge case first appeared in 1882 and is not the subject of a patent because it simply consists of a thin brass tube in the place of the laminated paper that was then the standard cartridge case.

This seemingly trifling alteration was really quite significant. The most immediate and obvious change was that here was a cartridge case that was unaffected by damp. Only those who have struggled with swollen cases as birds stream overhead can truly appreciate what a boon this is.

More subtle is the fact that, owing to the thinness of the case walls, the dimensions of the wads and the capacity of the case is altered. Ultimately it was found that barrels specially adapted to the 'Perfect' produced the best results from the innovation. Most of the improvement can be attributed to the virtual elimination of the forcing cone so that no longer were shot charges squeezed and compressed by the peak pressure of the propellant as they moved from cartridge to barrel. In this context, it is significant that William Ford advocated long forcing cones in guns that were intended to shoot Perfects. It is, therefore, something of a mystery why 20,000 shots reported such excellent results in guns that were intended for paper cases. The most likely explanation is the excellent quality of the wadding that he used.

Amid all the contemporary enthusiasm for the Perfect, it is noticeable that this was not shared completely by J.H. Walsh.

He, while praising the waterproof feature, seems otherwise unimpressed – an insight into the fact that he did not fully share Arthur Lane's central belief (not to say fixation!) with pattern quality.

Unsurprisingly, there were variants and changes made to the Perfect case. By special order, different lengths of case could be obtained. Later produced cases had strengthened bases and were adapted for a range of what were then called 'caps', what we now call 'primers'. Thus Winchester No 2 primers could be used in one variant, presumably to suit the American market. There were also cases made that accepted Berdan primers, while the standard paper case primer became the standard. This replaced the original primer with a long-legged anvil and was disapproved of by A.J. Lane who, in a letter to *The Field* of 28th April 1891, expressed the opinion that, by conducting the primer flash to the centre of the charge, the long-legged variant ensured better ignition of the powder charge.

While the manufacture of Perfect cases ceased in 1915, production was restarted briefly in 1920 of 3inch 12 bore cases.

A problem that emerged with extensive use of Perfects was that smokeless powder did not perform as well in them as it did in paper cases. The reason for this seems to be that, with smooth sides to the case and the style of closure used, it was not possible to ensure the confinement that nitro powder needed.

Many solutions to this problem suggest themselves, but I have yet to find in print if any were used. The closest I have yet seen is a note that, in their thin brass cases, the French fitted stronger caps. Lane's remark concerning the long-legged anvil is probably relevant here.

We, with the infinite wisdom conferred by hindsight, know that history has repeated itself, as is so often the way of things. Modern thin plastic-tubed cartridge cases have walls almost exactly the same thickness as a 'Perfect', but with the added advantage of being capable of being folded into a tight crimped closure, which both eliminates the overshot card wad and ensures the necessary confinement for the powder charge.

If these advantages are conserved, especially with top-quality wadding and barrels bored to suit, we should be able to exceed the performance of the 1880s.

KYNOCH & CO.,
AMMUNITION MANUFACTURERS.
MILITARY & SPORTING CARTRIDGES OF EVERY KIND.
PERCUSSION CAPS & WADDINGS.   FOG SIGNALS FOR RAILWAYS.

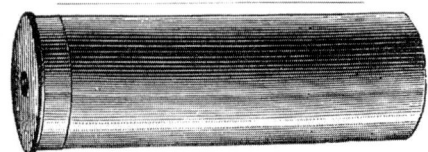

"PERFECT" CASE EMPTY.

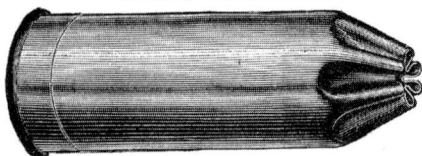

"PERFECT" CASE LOADED.

KYNOCH'S PATENT "PERFECT"
Central Fire and Pin Fire, 8, 10, 12, 14, 16, 20, 24, 28, ·410, and ·360 BORE
METALLIC CARTRIDGE.

NOTICE.

KYNOCH & CO. request buyers of the "Perfect" Cartridges to observe the new and effectual style of closing. It is impossible, under any circumstances, for the shot to get loose, or the wad to be displaced. Buyers of the No. 1 Crimper can have the Tool (necessary to complete the closing) gratis on application direct to our Works, at Witton, or from any of our Agents.

MISSFIRES having been found in some guns with weak springs, or imperfect locks, K. and Co. have now made the alterations necessary, and will guarantee that any gun in which the old paper cartridge can be used will answer for the "Perfect."

To show the advantage of the "Perfects" in guns made specially, we have a 28-bore gun (we will show to any one interested) which will hit and pierce an ordinary powder canister at 75 yards, the charge being only 2¾ drams of powder, and ¾ of an ounce of No. 4 shot. Guns of other bores, showing equally important improvements, may also be seen.

KYNOCH'S Patent Gas-tight Green and Salmon (for Schultze Powder; also Blue and Brown PAPER SPORTING CARTRIDGES in every size.
KYNOCH'S NICKEL-PLATED SPORTING CARTRIDGES.
KYNOCH'S SOLID METAL MARTINI-HENRY CARTRIDGES.
KYNOCH'S SOLID METAL EXPRESS CARTRIDGES.
KYNOCH'S SOLID METAL AND PAPER PUNT GUN CARTRIDGES.
KYNOCH'S ROOK RIFLE CARTRIDGES.
KYNOCH'S REVOLVER CARTRIDGES.

Illustrated Catalogue, Price List, and Samples forwarded to Merchants or Gunmakers on application to

KYNOCH & CO., WITTON, Near BIRMINGHAM.

THE NEW "PERFECT" SHELLS

"PERFECT" SHELLS! THERE was probably no more admirable hit ever made in the way of nomenclature than this, for truly there can be no doubt that these shells are as near perfection in their line as anything can be well expected to be, and are probably as great an advance in the art of gunning as the copper cap over the old flint, the breech-loader over the muzzle gun, or even the choke itself. A great deal has been written upon them, and a vast deal more said, and yet there appears to be a great deal of misunderstanding among shooters as to what their real advantages are, so that probably the following observations upon them from one wholly uninterested, and we hope equally unprejudiced in any way, may not be unacceptable to your readers.

The first point that suggests itself for consideration is – What is really to be got out of them in the guns made for paper shells, and secondly, in guns built especially for their use? With reference to the first category the editor of the *Field* says he can see no advantage in their use in these guns beyond the fact of their passing so easily in or out of the chambers on a wet day. This, we confess, puzzles us, as in every gun of the many tried by ourselves, we have in every case found an increase in pattern and also in force, but above all a great improvement in the evenness and distribution of the pattern, a wild shot being a very rare occurrence; and we cannot but think that the editor, in arriving at that conclusion, must have been singularly unlucky in the guns or the cartridges he used, or that he must somehow have overlooked the improvement in the regularity of the patterns obtained – in our opinion, *the* great and crowning advantage of these admirable shells. We ourselves think little of the small increase obtained in force or pattern, the old chokes shooting hard enough and close enough in all reason with the old paper shells; in fact, far too close for the great majority of shooters; but it is in the beauty and evenness of the pattern wherein consist the great advantages of these shells, and we think we need say no more with reference to their use out of old guns, as it is, undoubtedly, in guns built especially for them that their enormous advantages shew to the greatest perfection.

It will be necessary to go slightly into the question of bores and construction with reference to guns built specially for their use, before entering on the shooting to be obtained. The bore of the gun for the No. 12 case will be about 11; for the 14, 13 (the bore of the old 12 gun, for paper case); the 16, 15; the 20, 18; the 24, 21; and the 28, 24. These bores, no doubt, may vary from time to time a few thousandths of an inch larger or smaller, to suit the peculiar idiosyncrasies of the gun (to get up the shooting), or of the different makers, but that is of very small consequence to the owner, inasmuch as the gun will be regulated with waddings that fit the shells. The case is different with converted guns, as will be explained hereafter. With regard to the shooting to be obtained from these which we have previously designated Kynoch guns, it is perfectly marvellous, and every prophecy which we ventured to make on our first trial of these shells when they were first advertised, and before a gun had been specially made for them, has been amply and completely verified, and the elimination of the cone and shoulder in front of the chamber has not only increased the pattern, but has also almost entirely done away with "wild" shots. We will now compart the results to be obtained with both, that is, the gun bored for paper shells and for "Perfects."

PAPER SHELLS

In this form the construction of the cone a vast number of shot get jammed out of shape in passing, and nearly one-fourth of the whole charge does not reach the target at 40 yards.

A 12-shell gun of the best quality and full choke, with the No. 6 shot, will put on an average pattern of about 220, on the 30-inch circle, and a few shots outside it.

In force this gun will reach 2·00, 2·20 or thereabouts.

In the matter of wild shots, the average here can be scarcely considered less than one in 25 shots.

With the paper shells the patterns are almost invariably unequal, with clusters of three, four or more pellets close together, and wide thin spaces often so large that a bird might escape though held straight "on," and the outer edges of the circle much thinner than the centre, with often three or four such blank spaces in a pattern.

"PERFECT" SHELLS

With these only about 3 per cent of the charge is lost, the rest all going on to the target, and from the fact of all striking with a nearly equal force shews that they are not jammed out of shape.

A 12-shell Kynoch gun can be got to put on about 280, and nearly all the rest of the charge outside.

A 12-shell Kynoch gun will do about the same, but as the bores decrease in size, a considerable increase in force will be got over the other guns with the same sized shells, that is, a 16-shell Kynoch will materially beat a 16 paper, and a 20 still more so, and so on.

Here the wild shots amount to a fraction, under one in 300. It is true several shots might be found thin, but still with a pattern so evenly distributed that a bird could not escape, and could not, therefore, be classed with the wild.

The pattern here is most beautifully evenly distributed, nearly every pellet standing out single by itself, the edges of the circle being nearly as close and killing as the centre. We have shot for half-a-day with a good gun of this description without having a pattern with a space in it that a bird could escape through.

The above facts are collated from the results of nearly 1,800 shots fired by ourselves or under our direction, with the "Perfect" shells, and may be fully relied on; as, though we are incapable of writing or reading the largest print, we can still see sufficiently to hit a target at forty yards, and count and compare the results, and we think the above is quite sufficient to prove incontestably the vast advantages of the Kynoch gun over the old gun for paper shells, and we cannot imagine any one aware of these facts ever giving an order for the old guns.

We will now refer to the vexed question of converting old guns to the use of "Perfect" shells, on which there has been so much discussion. The system of bushing the chambers we do not at all approve. We have never seen any in which the gun was not weakened at its already weakest point. There is also the consideration of scoring and corrosion between the two cylinders, which appears to us to be inevitable when the bush is screwed in. Of the two, the bush had better be soldered in, in the old manner; but we infinitely prefer the system previously advocated by us of removing the shoulder, as has been done in our own guns, and can see no element of danger whatever in the proves, inasmuch as the metal still left is thicker than the barrel ever was at the end of the chamber. The shooting to be obtained in this manner is a vast increase in every way over the paper shells, though not equal to that of a gun built specially for them; but this could hardly be expected. What results may be expected from the bushing system we cannot say, never having had an opportunity of trying a gun so treated, but in over a dozen guns in which the shoulders were removed, tried by ourselves, the results were quite uniform, and even satisfactory. At the same time we think the process of removing the shoulder should only be entrusted to experienced hands, as no doubt barrels may occasionally be found bored out so much at this part in regulating their shooting for the paper shell as to be almost dangerously thin. It would obviously be foolish and risky to touch these, but in this case it would be almost certain to be wholly unnecessary, as the constriction at the shoulder would be so slight that the gun would be pretty certain to shoot well with the "Perfect" shells, as a short, abrupt cone appears to us to be the most fatal condition of a barrel for these shells. In having a gun bored for these shells as above suggested, the bore of the barrel being really too small for the shell, the load has frequently to be made o accommodate the barrel, and the diameter of the wadding used is of the greatest consequence as if too tight or too slack the effect will be immediately apparent on the plate. The borer should therefore send the owner the exact diameter in thousandths of an inch of the waddings used, and Messrs. Kynoch will, I know from experience, furnish the wadding of the exact size, but there can be no question, where a few pounds is not a consideration, it is far better to have a new pair of barrels fitted to the gun.

A good deal has been said about snaps in the use of these shells; our own experience of this disagreeable occurrence has been confined to four only, out of the large number of shells used by us, both new; and reloaded; these all four arose with new shells in the same barrel, in a gun of our own, in one morning's trial shooting. On examining the gun we found, as we anticipated, the fault lay solely here, as the striker in this barrel was considerably shorter than in the other; this was soon rectified, and there has been no recurrence of the evil, and we believe that where snaps have occurred, it has been wholly the fault of the guns, and not of the "Perfect" shells, and we trust that the outcry raised in this respect will not induce the manufacturers to substitute a more or too sensitive cap, which might some day lead to accidental discharges in or out of the gun. We are aware that they have already given up one great element of safety, in deference to the wishes of certain makers, viz., that of sinking the head of the cap a few hundredths of an inch below the surface of the end of the shells. The peculiar safety of this proceeding could hardly be over-estimated, but as the makers did not make their strikers long enough to ensure the discharge, Messrs. Kynoch gave up the practice. We hope, however, that nothing will induce them to make further concessions in this dangerous direction.

There was always to our mind a fatal objection to the old stout brass shells so much used in America. This was the very large cap employed in them. On the appearance of the first advertisement of the "Perfect," we saw by the woodcut that this great fault was cured, and we immediately wrote to Messrs. Kynoch for further information regarding them. This, though we were a perfect stranger, elicited a courteous replay, accompanied by a few shells, caps, anvils, and waddings, and we were delighted to find that the flash hole was no larger than in the paper shells; and, moreover, that more than half of this hole was occupied by the long square leg of the anvil passing through it. Thus not only was the large cap and the enormously increased flash from it in the old brass shell entirely done away with, but the smaller amount of flame from the reduced cap in the "Perfects" was partially blocked by the leg of the anvil, and the flash divided into four small jets, thus preventing the too rapid combustion of the charge of powder; and herein, in our opinion, lies one of the principal factors in obtaining the marvellous regularity in shooting.

Our first trials of the "Perfects" at the place lasted nearly two days firing as rapidly as we could reload, count, and record the shots, and after firing a few shots with the proper load for the gun, and ascertaining that the shooting was in every respect a considerable advance on anything previously got out of the gun, we devoted ourselves to testing their durability. For this purpose we fired a great number of rounds with the heaviest loads of powder, and both large and small shot, that we could cram into a 12-shell; in fact, loads we could never have ventured on except in a cross-bolt-actioned gun, without the certainty of a gaping joint, if nothing worse. We shot till our shoulder and cheek were black. The shells, after five-and-twenty or thirty rounds of such loads, were as good as at first; and, in fact, we have never yet succeeded in spoiling one of them even by such unfair use; and one correspondent of the *Field*, a professional shooter, has lately written that he has reloaded them 500 times, so that they may be considered practically almost indestructible. Our own practice, however, is, as they are so reasonable in price, to throw them away after firing, as we did the paper, as we avoid the trouble of re-capping, slight as it is, and we dislike a number of empty shells in the pocket; but it is impossible to overestimate the advantages of this remarkable durability to those shooting in remote districts – in India, or elsewhere, where a man may wait for even months for a relay of ammunition. We have recommended them to all our friends – especially those going abroad – and one gallant major of our acquaintance will take out 2,000 of them on his return to India.

The re-capping process is the most easy and simple possible; the exploded cap and anvil can be pushed out with any common stick cut with a flat end; to return the anvil, put a new cap over it, and press it down home with the handle of a pocket turnscrew, is but the work of a few seconds, and after loading, the corrugated pattern of crimper may be readily and effectually carried out with a strong thumb nail, or the side edge of the blade of a pocket turnscrew, or even a shilling will do the work, as we know from experience; so that the whole re-loading process can be carried out even in the field without extra impedimenta.

The other advantages may be speedily summed up. They are, of course, wholly unaffected by any climate or weather; the smoke, is using black powder, is perceptibly less than with paper, and they will bear any amount of tumbling or knocking about when loaded, without the smallest injury to their effectiveness in the gun; and we can, therefore, most thoroughly recommend their use to all our brother sportsmen.

There has hitherto been a singular amount of opposition to them from various quarters. This we can only account for on the principle that the better a thing is the more it is opposed. It will be recollected that even Joe Manton set his face steadfastly against the percussion system, and was to the last but a half-hearted convert.

What opposition did Laing find when he first took up breechloaders in 1851! And even now, with regard to chokes, there are still makers to be found who will not turn them out unless insisted on by their customers. Nevertheless, we venture to predicate a long and complete success to the "Perfect" shells.

BY ONE WHO HAS FIRED SOME 20,000 TRIAL SHOTS AT MARKS

THE SPORTING MIRROR, 1st half of 1891 (Page 287)

Ford's Cartridges

William Ford and the guns he made are topics which crop up right through the various writings of Arthur Lane. We must, therefore, assume that Arthur Lane was a customer and probably a friend of William Ford. They certainly had interests in common, especially barrel boring and ballistics.

WILLIAM FORD,
MAKER OF THE ECLIPSE DOUBLE GUN
(Weight under 4lb.)
Guarantees to give any pattern up to 200 with 1oz. of shot, 270 to oz.
Price from 15 Guineas up to 35 Guineas.
Borer of the winning guns at Field Trials, London, 1875 and 1879. Highly recommended by "20,000 Shots;" with Gold Medal and Certificate.
W. F. guarantees to improve any Gun from $\frac{7}{16}$ up to 2in. in the bore on the "Eclipse" system of Boring. (See reports of above, August 1st and 15th, highly recommended by the Editor of the SHOOTING TIMES.)
Terms:—Cash with Order.
$4\frac{1}{2}$, WEAMAN ROW, ST. MARY'S, BIRMINGHAM.

Thus, it is unsurprising that the following endorsement appeared in *The Field* of July 31st 1897:

FORD PATENT CARTRIDGES

I feel certain when Mr. Ford's cartridges get well known they will entirely supersede the old cases, and revolutionise the present system of loading. I was perfectly astonished and may add that, in my opinion, these shells will turn out to be the greatest improvement devised for many years.

20,000 shots

Patent No. 17073 of 1896

The cartridge case in question is presumably that covered in patent No. 17,073 of 1896, the features of which were the central ignition of the powder charge, the cup-shaped powder chamber and the shoulders on the chamber to prevent crushing the charge.

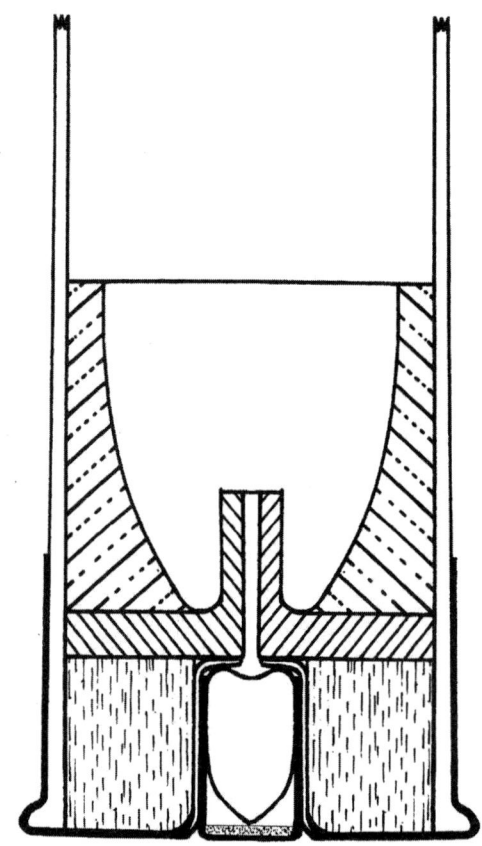

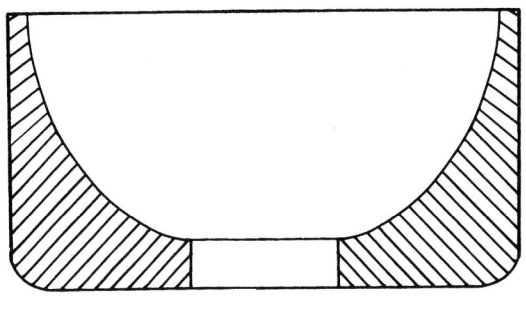

Patent No. 19440 of 1890

The cup-shaped base wad had, in fact, been the subject of an earlier W. Ford patent, No. 19,440 of 1890, and is the design that is in very wide use in plastic cartridge cases today.

NOTE from *The Field* of August 25th 1883, Page 288:

William Ford had a range "six steps" from his workshop door with a set of hinged plates actuated by wires so that a series of five shots could be fired each at a fresh plate.

This, in the centre of Birmingham.

'The Guns of our Ancestors' Trial

It is a feature of this trial, despite claims to the contrary, that it was not preceded by a series of readers' letters on the subject. Indeed, reading all that was printed, it is hard to escape the suspicion that it owed its origins to an editorial idea.

Again, we have the participation of Arthur Lane, and this time he had a more prominent role. Moreover, three guns from his collection were included in the line-up, together with, amongst others, three guns of wider historical significance. There were two guns once used by Col. Hawker – alas not his Mantons, but a Burnett and a Westley Richards – and also the Lancaster double flint gun, which remained in the Lancaster collection until comparatively recent times.

Valid criticisms can be made of some of the methodology of the trial. Should percussion ignition guns originally bored as flintlocks have been included with guns specifically designed for percussion ignition and should only one load have been used for the tests? On this point it could have been highly illuminating to have a record of the loads that the gun owners chose to use as a result of their own tests and field experience.

On this note, it is worthy of comment that Arthur Lane's brother's gun, the Harding single barrel 16 bore, came to the trial with the reputation of being "a remarkably good gun to kill", but, in fact, it failed to produce a pattern of 100 pellets in a 30inch circle at 40 yards. This must equate to a broader than average pattern at closer ranges, which could well have been the foundation of its reputation.

The following letter in *The Field* of 22nd March 1890 is relevant here:

> ……..On one occasion my brother and myself both using single guns one day in October on a farm called Busses in Sussex got thirty six shots and carried home thirty three head – a mixed bag; and I think my brother killed eighteen in succession missing his nineteenth and last shot.
>
> On another occasion I found myself with a friend without a gun, so it was agreed we should use his in turn. It was a light 12 bore with 30inch barrels. I am not quite certain whether we had twenty-three or twenty-seven shots but whichever it was we neither of us made a miss.

Part of a longer letter. Another story follows in much the same vein.

The question of the load to be used in the trial was evidently one of some difficulty for the organisers and they did preliminary trials with a range of options. Interestingly, in the process we learn that A.J.L. and his brother used 2 or 2½ drms of very fine powder (TSI), crumpled brown paper for a wad and 1¼ or 1½ oz of shot in the 16 bore gun.

In the event, wool felt wads were used, both because they were acknowledged as the best but also because they were akin to the wads cut from old beaver hats, which had been used in the 18th century.

The preliminary trials had yielded the fact that fine powder was indeed the best for the guns, so a standard charge of 2 drms was fixed and, with this, no less than 1¼ oz of No. 6 shot was used.

If this shot load seems excessive to modern thinking, it was after all in line with the load quoted by Arthur Lane and also, it must be observed, less than some 18th century sources advocated.

Taken as a whole, the trial was a rare example of an attempt at a scientific appraisal of the performance of a muzzle loading shotgun.

The results of the trial and the guns shot can be summarised as follows:

THE GUNS SHOT IN THE 'GUNS OF OUR ANCESTORS' TRIAL:

FLINTLOCKS:

SEGALAS - Single 11 Bore*. Length of barrel – 32ins.
Diameter of the bore, breech ·736; at 18ins from breech ·725. Cylindrical for 4ins then relieved to muzzle where diameter was ·744.
Pattern 119, three shots balled.
Average velocity below 640 feet/sec the lowest reading on chronograph.

MORTIMER – Double 16 Bore*. Length of barrel – 30ins.
Diameters of the bores, right barrel ·654 at breech, tapering to ·653 at muzzle. Left barrel ·649 at breech and for next 17ins then tapering to ·652 at muzzle.
Pattern 133, one shot balled. (Entire charge in three clusters)
Velocity, right barrel 736 feet/sec, left barrel 740 feet/sec.

LANCASTER – Double 11 Bore. Length of barrels 31ins.
Diameters of bores, right barrel ·753 at breech tapering to ·75 at 29ins from breech, cylindrical to ·751 at muzzle. Left barrel, ·753 at breech tapering to ·751 at 28ins from breech, cylindrical to ·751 at muzzle.
Pattern 147.
Velocity, right barrel 743feet/sec, left barrel 734 feet/sec.

PERCUSSION IGNITION GUNS:

DICKSON – Double 20 Bore. Length of barrels 27½ins.
 Diameter of bores, right barrel ·611 at breech, ·610 ½in from breech, cylindrical for 6ins then opening to ·612 at muzzle. Left barrel, ·614 at breech, ·610 ½in from breech, cylindrical for 5ins then opening to ·12 at muzzle.
 Pattern 99.
 Velocity 755 feet/sec.

HARDING – Single 16 Bore*. Length of barrel 27¾ins.
 Diameter of bore ·670 at breech tapering to ·664 at 21¾ins from breech, opening to ·671 at muzzle.
 Pattern 94.
 Velocity 755feet/sec.

JOE MANTON – Double 20 Bore*, converted from flint. Length of barrels 31ins.
 Diameters of barrels, right barrel ·600 at breech tapering to ·599 at 10ins from breech, Cylindrical for next 18ins, opening to ·607 in last 3ins. Left barrel ·601 at breech, ·600 at 9ins from breech, cylindrical for next 13 ins, then opening to ·607 at muzzle.
 Patterns – right barrel 110, left barrel 117.
 Velocity – right barrel 718 feet/sec, left barrel 748 feet/sec.

WESTLEY RICHARDS – Double 12 Bore. Length of barrels 31ins.
 Diameters of bores, right barrel ·714 at breech tapering to ·707 at 26ins from breech, then opening to ·720 at muzzle. Left barrel ·712 at breech, tapering to ·706 at 26ins from breech, the opening to ·720 at muzzle.
 Patterns – right barrel 120, left barrel 125.
 Velocity – right barrel 735 feet/sec, left barrel 715 feet/sec.

BURNETT – Double 12 Bore. Length of barrels 33ins.

Diameter of bores, right barrel ·725 at breech, tapering to ·723 at 24ins from breech, cylindrical for 6ins then opening to ·730 at muzzle. Left barrel ·725 at breech, tapering to ·723 at 27ins from breech, cylindrical for 3ins then opening to ·727 at muzzle.

Patterns – right barrel 143, left barrel 128.

Velocity – right barrel 734 feet/sec, left barrel 774 feet/sec.

NOTES:
- *Indicates a gun owned by A.J. Lane.
- Pattern is the average of six shots, the number pellets in 30in circle at 40 yards.
- The velocities quoted are the average over 40 yards and equate to muzzle velocities of less than 900 feet/sec.

The most important fact demonstrated by this event, but curiously not really given due prominence, was the vital importance of effective wadding and how its absence frequently resulted in the shot fusing together in the barrel and balling. This was passed over as a mere failure of the pattern, but the danger of the lethal projectile, capable of inflicting severe wounds well beyond the range of loose shot, is left aside.

In addition, the trial induced me to see how the muzzle loading gun that I have shot extensively both at clays and game compared. Wary of the seductive trap of seeking the perfect load, I simply tested one barrel with the load I habitually shoot.

Guns, Gun Barrels and Gunmaking

It was inevitable that the design of the gun should be part of Lane's obsession with ballistics and so it could be argued that a separate section is an artificial division. While this is true, it is necessary to create some sort of logical consideration.

Unsurprisingly, the style of gun advocated by Arthur Lane was the product of his style of shooting, the vast majority of which was walked up and, in his later years, walking up in open country where long shots were the rule.

Thus it was that Lane, along with most other authors who have written about shooting walked up game, was an advocate of light guns. Indeed, the late Roger Barlow went further. It was his firmly held view that, for shooting Bob White quail, there was no such thing as a gun that was too light!

Coupled with a light weight, Lane was also an advocate of short barrels. Today these are inextricably linked to Robert Churchill and his advocacy of 25-inch barrels in the 1920s and '30s. We have no means of knowing if Churchill simply rediscovered the virtues of short barrels or if he was aware of Lane's writings of 50 years before.

It is a measure of A.J.L.'s standing that his views were deemed to have commercial value as the following letter shows:

A SHORT BARRELLED 16 BORE.

SIR: Your correspondence "John Halifax" in his reply to "Durham", I note omits to give any figures that show the difference between long and short barrelled 16 bores when shot for pattern and penetration, which is the real test of a gun's shooting, as anyone conversant with plating guns and killing game is well aware.

If a gun fits a man, no matter how poor the shooting of the weapon, he will kill more game – and kill it clean too – than with a gun giving the finest pattern and penetration in the world that does not fit him.

I well remember when Eastwell Park was a Royal residence, one gentleman who was a frequent guest, standing well back, killing overhead pheasants that some people thought out of reach. Yet his cartridges (12 bores) were only loaded with 2¾drs of powder and 1oz of No. 6 and the average pattern of his gun was not over 100 with this load, but they fitted him and he held well forward, getting the birds in the middle of the charge.

To return to 16 bores, in 1879 I built for "One that has Fired 20,000 Shots at Marks" a 16 bore gun with barrels only 22in long weighing 5¾lb. It was shot with 2¾drs of coarse ground Basket powder and 1oz of No. 6 chilled shot and at 40 yards the pattern taken from an average of twenty five shots was 155.28 and the penetration 207.34. For comparison I will take the same 15 bore guns giving the highest figures of merit in the 1879 Field Trials, as they were shot about the same date and under similar conditions, but with this difference, that all these six guns with one exception, had barrels 30in long. Their combined averages were pattern 170.66, penetration 218.84.

From the above figures "Durham" will see that guns with barrels of only 22in can be made to shoot nearly as well as those with barrels of the full length. After receiving the gun "One who has Fired 20,000 shots at Marks" wrote me that the above figures had not done the little gun justice, as he had obtained higher results.

W.R. LEESON.
ASHFORD, KENT. FEB. 20.

THE FIELD, 23rd February 1895.

On the question of short barrels, it is a curious fact that writers in the 20th century claimed that short barrels were best suited to shooters of Robert Churchill's build – that is to say tending to the short and more rounded stature. Arthur Lane was six feet tall with broad shoulders and long arms!

Where Churchill and Lane differ is on the subject of the boring of the barrels, but this is easily explained by the fact that Churchill guns were designed for driven game, especially partridges, while Lane shot the same game under very different conditions.

Aside from these features, there are two other themes that run through A.J.L.'s writing on guns. First we have the crusade against, the final conversion and then the championing of steel gun barrels.

This story is told in a series of long letters to *The Field*, principally in 1884 and 1888, the references to which are to be found in Appendix 1.

Lane's opposition to steel as a barrel material derived from two sources. He was convinced that steel barrels did not throw as good a quality pattern as Damascus and he attributed this to the variations of hardness within the metal.

More seriously, he believed the contemporary steel to be dangerous and claimed to have seen numerous examples of shattered barrels. Of course, he lacked the facilities and the knowledge to elucidate the causes of these failures. Additionally, the provenance of the barrels was unknown to the owners of the guns.

All that A.J.L. could do was look at the fractures with a lens and, in this way, he claimed to have seen a crystalline structure. From this he came to believe that a process of crystallisation led to the embrittlement of the metal.

No matter what the cause, or causes, of this problem, his opposition to steel was an entirely pragmatic approach. Moreover, as he pointed out, the appearance of steel as a barrel material made possible all sorts of chicanery and deception since, when blacked, the worst looked just like the best. Indeed, blacking had even wider potential in that twist barrels could be repaired and then blacked to hide the deficiency, something that could not be done with browning where every fibre of the metal is visible.

On this last point, Arthur, like many other commentators before and since his time, pointed out that the quality of a Damascus barrel could be appraised by visual inspection - this despite the fact that the material existed in truly bewildering varieties. For instance, in 1897, one Liègois gunmaker offered thirty different types of Damascus barrel.

Against this background, it is entirely laudable that Arthur Lane showed himself prepared to move with the times and embrace advances in technology.

Thus we find the following letter in *The Field* of July 5th 1884:

STEEL BARRELS

SIR, It will doubtless be in the recollection of many of your readers that three or four years ago there was a considerable discussion in your columns as to the relative merits of these barrels as compared with mixed metals during which I expressed a strong opinion against steel founded on the irregular results obtained from the barrels turned out many years ago by the London Cold-drawn Steel Gun Barrel Company who had their factory in the Commercial Road, and I attributed this irregularity in shooting to the unequal degrees of hardness in the metal as interfering with the regular wave expansion set up by the discharge. This opinion I now wish to publicly withdraw as I have lately had an opportunity of trying a number of pairs of barrels made by Mr. Wm. Tranter of Lichfield Road, Birmingham and I must say better or more thoroughly even and more regular shooting from any set of guns it would be difficult to find. Mr. Tranter has long been well known as a first class maker of revolvers and rifles but has, I believe, only recently gone into the sporting trade. But the guns I tried (all of them 12 bores – some made to order, others for stock) were all of most excellent materials and finish, and would do credit, as well in this respect as for the shooting to the best known guns. Mr. Tranter, it appears, has become possessed of the plant and machinery formerly belonging to the old London company above referred to, and I lately saw it in operation. Whether it is that the steel of the present day is so much better and more homogenous than that of some thirty years ago, when the London company was in operation, or whether Mr. Tranter has a new mode of preparing and working it, I know not, but this is certain that he has in some way entirely overcome the defects before referred to, as nothing could be better or more even than the results I obtained, without exception from all of the barrels tried by me. There is another great advantage in his manufacture that these barrels are perfectly true on the outside, and in, so that when revolving from a centre both surfaces run without a "wobble" and when laid together and fired from a fixed rest both barrels deliver their shot perfectly concentrically on the target – a great advantage to the shooter. It was but a few weeks ago that I advised a friend to absolutely reject a gun making (sic) for him by one of our most eminent makers on account of the shots crossing, each barrel to the extent of six inches, thus putting one clear foot between them. This is quite enough to entail a clean miss, if say the left barrel were fired at a bird crossing to the left however good the aim, as the centre of the shot would be a clear foot behind the bird. I mention this to illustrate the immense advantage of having both barrels to shoot true to the centre – a matter too frequently overlooked by sportsmen. The enormous strength of these cold drawn steel barrels must also deserve comment and consideration. I am informed that a 12 bore barrel of the ordinary weight required a load of 27 drs of powder, two cork wads, and two bullets before it bulged and 55 drs etc before it burst. Such enormous strength and tenacity as this could I think not be found in any mixed metal. There still remains, however, the risk, unless dealing direct with a factory of such high and well known respectability as Mr. Tranter's of having common smoke brown barrels palmed off as true steel, there being no pattern to act as a guide, but I believe Mr. Tranter affixes his trade mark stamp on all barrels supplied by him. To make sure, however, I would recommend all sportsmen desiring these barrels to send their order for the gun direct to Lichfield Road, and I will answer for it, they will not be disappointed in what they get, in either work, material, or handiness.

One who has fired 20,000 trial shots at marks

Apart from its intrinsic interest, this letter is reproduced because it is a snapshot illustrating the rush of progress that was such a feature of the 19th century. Here we have a record of how a process was invented, found to produce an unsatisfactory product and then, thirty years later, advances in technology enabled the deficiencies to be corrected, proving the soundness of the original concept. Moreover, a product which was superior to anything available previously was placed on the market.

Today we see a similar march of technology in electronic gadgetry and can only envy Arthur Lane and his contemporaries who lived through a time when sporting guns evolved at such a pace.

How to Choose a Gun

This article was first published in *The Sporting Mirror*, Volume III, January to June 1882. At this time, A.J. Lane would have been sixty six years old. This piece merits reproduction by virtue of the many points and levels of interest that it contains, not least because the type of gun recommended is the diametric opposite of what is currently (2016) fashionable. In large part, this divergence can be explained by the different modes of shooting game. It is the variance which exists between walking all day for a few shots and being conveyed by wheeled transport to a succession of pegs and having a plentiful supply of high pheasants driven over.

On the wider issue of the evolution of the sporting gun, the date of this piece puts it in the period when the hammerless gun was far from universally accepted. One of the points urged against the hammerless gun is the peculiarly sensual pleasure of cocking a lock of the highest quality.

Besides all this, we have here, in the clearest possible terms, A.J. Lane's ideas and preferences in the choice of guns. So, above all, this is shooting autobiography.

HOW TO CHOOSE A GUN

THE CHOICE OF a gun, indeed, is a subject opening up questions that at first sight look interminable, but really and truly resolve themselves into a very simple matter of pretty easy solution. It is purely and simply a matter of individual taste, and as such it must ever remain.

The first point to be determined is what a man really likes and what he wants. Simple as this looks on paper, singularly enough, many mean are to be found who have proved utterly incapable of forming a correct judgment thereon. This question, however, is greatly one of weight; a man should well consider this, and it must not be what he can handle and pitch about just as he likes, with delectable ease, in a gunmaker's shop, but what he can comfortably *carry* (not *lug* about with him) for a long day's tramp of ten or a dozen hours, over a rough and heavy country. And this is a matter of the very highest importance; so surely as a man overweights himself in his gun, even but a little, so surely will his shooting go off as fatigue overtakes him till at last he can hardly hit a haystack, and he would do infinitely better in the long run if he carried a much smaller and lighter gun though not so good by ten yards. This question of weight controls greatly that of bore and length. There can be no question about it, that a twelve-bore gun is for all-round general game shooting far the best, most useful, and effective that can be carried, provided a man is equal to the weight; if not, it is far better to take to a sixteen at once, which will do all the ordinary work of the season, and as these can be built light enough in all reason, if not too long, they are greatly to be preferred to a twenty, as they shoot harder and give a larger killing circle at all ranges. None but a really good quick shot, in fact "a crack," should venture on a twenty-bore as they are of little use over forty yards unless full choked, in which case the killing circle is very small, some twenty-five to twenty-seven inches at forty yards, which requires very close shooting; but in really good hands they are fearfully deadly on account of the great ease with which they can at all times be handled. A table of weights to which guns of various lengths can be safely made will be found hereafter, which may be useful to many shooters.

The next point that presents itself for consideration is that of length, and this again is purely a matter of taste; if a man likes a short, light gun, by all means have it. It is now thoroughly demonstrated by the guns turned out by some few makers who will take the trouble to please their customers in this respect, that short barrels are not one whit behind the normal thirty and twenty-eight inches, in either strength or pattern, and at all events shoot well enough. And the enormous advantages of a short gun over a long one, in the rapidity and ease with which it can be got "on" the object, and the great facility and comfort in handling, especially in covert or in hot weather, can only be duly appreciated by those who have used them through the vicissitudes of several seasons. The writer can hardly get a gun too short or too light for him, and has, during the last forty years, possessed and exclusively shot with, a considerable number varying from twenty-two to twenty-six inches long, weighing from five pounds three ounces to six pounds and from twelve to twenty-two bores the whole of which (with one exception) have been not only up to average shooting, but have been in most cases quite level with the best of their gauges of twenty-eight and thirty inches long. But twenty-four inches is considered, by the writer, about the best and most convenient for a twelve, twenty-five for a sixteen, and for a twenty bore twenty-six inches is better, the very narrow bore requiring a greater length, or some of the powder *may* be liable to be blown out unburnt unless a load is employed too small to obtain the proper force. It must, however, be borne in mind that a man who carries a light gun of any bore must be prepared to feel more recoil than with a heavy one, but it is a fact that among the very large number of guns that have been tried by the writer, almost all cases of extraordinarily good shooting, beyond the average, have occurred with guns with *light thin* barrels, and it is believed that as a rule light barrels do shoot the best.

Nothing is said here of larger bores; they may be very good for flock shooting, but, in fact, unless a ten-bore is so heavy as to take very large loads of heavy shot, it is *certain* to be beaten by any really good twelve (they ought not to be much under eight and a-half pounds to be of any good); and this great weight renders them much too cumbersome and fatiguing for a tramp after game, and quite inadmissible on even only a warm day. They may do very well for the pigeon shooter, who only *stands* for an hour or two at the traps. But most men who are fair shots would no doubt kill more game throughout a season and with half the fatigue, with a light, handy twelve or sixteen, as they then shoot as well towards evening as at the start.

Weights to which guns can be built to be perfectly safe and shoot well will be found at the end of this paper.

The next great point in a gun is to get one to thoroughly "fit." And that is often a really difficult matter, on account of the very different manner in which many men handle a gun in a maker's shop to what they do in the field; others entirely ignore the question of fatigue (a fatal mistake) and think there is no such a thing as getting tired; hence they overweight themselves and inevitably spoil their shooting in the afternoons, when the most sport may usually be looked for, while some unhappy individuals appear to be in a most perfect state of blissful ignorance as to what does and what does not suit them. These last cases are pretty nearly hopeless unless they happen to fall into the hands of a really clever, skilful mast gunmaker himself. The assistants you usually find in gunmakers' shops are generally most civil and obliging fellows, excellent workmen, who fully understand the whole work and mechanism of a gun and are first-class "viewers," but are woefully behind in the art of seeing what really suits a man and what he can shoot with; in fact, it is a rare exception that a man is an adept at this unless he is himself a practical shooter, not a mere trier of guns at the plate.

A very large percentage of gunmakers, in my opinion, make their guns much too crooked and too long in the stock, and worse than this, make the comb of the gun so nearly in the plane of the top rib that it can fit none but very short-necked men, whereas to get a really handy gun the bump should drop considerably lower. Generally from the bump being kept so high, the toe (lower point of the heel plate), and the toe only with most men, comes to the shoulder instead of the very centre of the heel plate, where it not only digs into the shoulder most unpleasantly at every shot, but gives but a poor, unstable, rickety support to the gun, which wabbles (sic) about either way, instead of the firm, steady, immovable hold which the centre of the heel gives when pressed firmly to the shoulder; and no man can shoot his best with such a fit. It will be seen that a bend with a low bump really comprises the benefits of both a straight and a crooked stock, as it is not only much straighter at the "face," the point of the greatest importance of all, and which *alone* determines the "lay" of the gun to the eye, but the greater angle to lower the bump brings, as before stated, the *centre* of the heel plate broadly and flatly on to the shoulder, and at the same time reduces the feeling of recoil; therefore, the two great points to be looked to in fitting a man with a gun are, first, to ascertain the exact bend at the face, and secondly, to determine the angle of the comb to the plane of the barrels so that without altering the face the bump shall drop so that the very centre of the heel plate comes to the shoulder, and all other points in the shape of the stock are of little or no consequence whatever. The questions of "cast off" and the most ready means of finding the band, length, &c., must now claim our attention. It must be borne in mind that the more crooked the stock the longer it must be, to keep the muzzle up at all; and both these tend enormously to increase the unhandiness of the gun, and rapidity of action is almost impossible with it. Again, if the balance is bad – too heavy at either end (one is as bad as the other) – a man cannot expect to perform beyond mediocrity. But all these matters, it may be said, resolve themselves into points of personal taste, though this is really much less so than many may imagine. If a man's gun has too much bend, as is most often the case, it is easily found out. Take a piece of wood, say 6in. or 7in. long, ⅜in. thick, and ½in. or ⅝in. deep; hollow out the bottom edge of it till it (fairly) fits the top of the comb of the gun, then cut out a piece ½in. square at each end, leaving two projections at the bottom. By these bind it firmly on to the gunstock on the top of the comb, taking care to take a turn or two round the heel plate to prevent the bindings slipping forward; then proceed to cut or rasp away the top, until reduced to shat is thought to be the right band, but stop at such a point that when the gun is thrown quickly up and the cheek pressed to the stock the eye cannot be got lower than that an imaginary line from the eye to the "sight" at the muzzle shall pass half an inch or so *above* the break-off. With a gun so laid a bird got on the point of it at a moderate distance is almost certain to go over. But if the band is so great that the top of the break-off and sight are readily brought into a line, the excitement of shooting almost invariably causes it to drop below; and when the sight is once lost there is no telling whether the muzzle is half an inch or half a foot below the object. Not that this is a matter of much consequence, as the smaller variation is quite enough to insure a clean miss. In arriving at this bend the assistance of a competent friend or a gunmaker may be had recourse to, presenting the gun (first seeing that the barrels are empty) at his eye. But a far better plan is that which I have employed for many years and which I first made public in the *Field* some time since; that is, place yourself before a good sized looking-glass and aim at your own eye, raising the gun repeatedly, steadily, but quickly, as in shooting at a bird. Note that there is no jerk when the heel plate settles on to the shoulder; if it does so it will probably be seen that the muzzle describes a small irregular circle. No one can shoot with a gun that does this. It usually arises from the stock being too long or too short. This can be ascertained by placing a pad in the sleeve of the jacket. If the gun is too short the evil will be cured, if too long it is increased, and the experiment of removing the heel plate can be tried for shortening. The next thing is to see how the muzzles fall on the eye. If the smallest particle of the top of the barrels or top rib can be seen it is *certain* the gun will be under everything. If the barrels come so that nothing is seen but the two round holes, it may be theoretically correct; but in practice and the hurry of shooting it will be quite as often under as not. But when the muzzles are perfectly steady when the gun is quickly thrown up, and the under side of the barrels is just seen all the way down to where the left hand grasps the fore end, depend on it the gun will be found to be all right; in which case a careful drawing or "jig" (model) of the bend shall be made, with all the measures accurately taken (this, if unaccustomed to such work, will be better done by a gunmaker), and have the gun stocked to this pattern. Always keep such jig or pattern by you in case of meeting with an accidental break, as you are then sure of getting the gun re-stocked as it was. Another fruitful source of misfit in guns is the amount of "cast off," and here arises the point of whether a man shoots with both eyes open, as every man should do who wishes to perform in really good style. Should he, however, close the left eye, he will probably do best if the gun is not cast off at all or very slightly. The proper amount depends on the width between the eyes and manner of holding the head of each individual shooter. It is easy enough to see if it is right. Look down the gun and see if the line of sight passes directly over the very middle of the break-off to the sight on the muzzle; if it should appear to be either to the right or left of such exact centre, it is a sign that the stock is cast off too much or too little. Or a small piece of thin paper may be shut into the "joint," in which cut a narrow V to form a temporary back sight; this will shew at once any error in the "casting off," as the "sight" should of course fall exactly *in* it, on throwing the gun to the shoulder. This plan is invaluable in fitting a cross-eyed gun for a left-eyed man.

There are many other points for consideration in the choice of a gun, as to make, material, actions, &c., but these are greatly matters of individual liking; but as probably an opinion might be desired on some of these matters it may be said that a very considerable experience induces the writer to say nothing is so good and durable for barrels as first-class Laminated steel. Next in order comes Damascus and silver steel Damascenes, certainly handsomer patterns to look at, but hardly so strong (weight for weight) as Laminated steel, on account of the fibre of the metal not running so directly in the direction of the strain. Much has lately been said of the excellence of some of the modern steel barrels, but it is a matter that at best has not been fully tried or proved. One great objection is, it can never be *seen* what they are, consequently no moderately low-priced gun can be trusted, or any, indeed, unless bought of makers of very high stamp for integrity, and even they are to a certain extent at the mercy of their barrel makers, despite the care they themselves may bestow on the working. And if fraud is intended nothing is so easy. The smoke browning generally applied to steel barrels will not only admit of the covering up of an unlimited amount of greys flaws, specks, &C., but will effectually conceal the most villainous skelp barrels that can be made. Of Belgian barrels little need be said; they are usually very pretty to look at, but so soft and bad that no one should ever think for a moment of buying a gun in which they have been made up, whether choke or cylinder, as they can never be depended on for holding their shooting for even one season. Of action, those that are made with elongations of the top rib with a top bolt, whether across it or into a "doll head," are unquestionably by far the most durable, best, and strongest. In speaking of locks we open up the question of hammerless guns. Whether the present craze for them will really last may be a moot question; they are certainly, the best of them, exceedingly ugly, having exactly the appearance of a cropped cat, and the confounded bolt, whether automatic or not, is mostly the wrong way, and is a constant source of risk, vexation, and annoyance. The writer has used one constantly during a *whole* season, a most excellent little gun, but the advantages have yet to be discovered. In an experience of over fifty years of no feather-bed shooting, chiefly in, perhaps some of the wildest of countries and roughest of covers to be found in England, I have never yet lost a shot by handing up the hammer of a gun or found anything more than a leaf or two clinging in them, or ever experienced the slightest inconvenience, or seen any accident whatever arising from them. It may be an old-fashioned idea, but to me there is a very great pleasure in manipulating a really good pair of locks during a day's shooting, and it can always be so readily seen at a glance what condition the gun is in that there is no possible excuse for a mistake; and though it may require some courage in the present day and general state of feeling among sportsmen, I cannot but record my deliberate opinion that nothing has yet ever been brought out so good and so thoroughly safe and reliable in every respect as the modern rebounding locks. To those, therefore (and I believe these are many) who, like myself, prefer rebounding locks, a few words may be said as to bar and back actions. If a gun is intended for real work and knocking about, especially abroad, there can be no question which is the best. The back action gun, too, can be made twice as strong, and one-third lighter, or thereabouts, than with bar locks – two enormous advantages; but the *wood* in the "hand" is perhaps slightly stronger with bar locks. Bar locks look very nice and do very well for the fashionable shooter, who stands for a couple of hours or so at the end of a cover and blazes away as hard as he can, and whose gun does not get really a day's *rough* work throughout a season. But for the real working sportsman who keeps his guns for work, and not to be looked at, the back action locks are undoubtedly the strongest and best, and it is believed, weight for weight, are stronger than most of the hammerless guns now out – many of them being so much cut away in the "body" for the locks, but no doubt most of them are even stronger than an ordinary bar lock breechloader. If a hammerless gun is chosen, see that it has the locks *on plates*, so that they can be readily got at, taken off for cleaning or examination should anything get wrong. Any gun requiring a vice and drifting tools to get at the inside of the locks is an utter abomination, that no sportsman should look at twice. And there is but one bolt of the whole lot automatic (so called), or otherwise, that I consider worth a "rap," and in my opinion, no hammerless gun is safe without it. In point of act, I fancy this bolt leaves nothing to be desired in the way of either safety or handiness, and too much cannot be said in its favour. I certainly never liked *any* hammerless guns till I got it, the old confounded bolts being nearly always the wrong way in spite of the greatest care – "off" when you wanted safety and "on" when you wanted to fire. Now, I must admit that I am so far converted that at this time I am having built for me another hammerless gun; this gun is to be specially chambered for the Kynoch's new "perfect" shell, a most valuable invention, and which will no doubt revolutionise gunmaking ere long.

Twelve Bores.

	lb.	oz.		lb.	oz.
22-inch barrels...	2	14	24-inch barrels...	3	0
Fore end ...	0	4	Fore end ...	0	4
Butt ...	2	6	Butt ...	2	8
	5	8		5	12

	lb.	oz.		lb.	oz.
26-inch barrels...	3	2	28 inch barrels...	3	4
Fore end ...	0	4	Fore end ...	0	4
Butt ...	2	10	Butt ...	2	12
	6	0		6	4

Sixteen Bores.

	lb.	oz.		lb.	oz.
22-inch barrels...	2	8	24-inch barrels...	2	11
Fore end ...	0	3	Fore end ...	0	3
Butt...	2	5	Butt ...	2	6
	5	0		5	4

	lb.	oz.		lb.	oz.
26-inch barrels...	2	13	28-inch barrels...	2	15
Fore end ...	0	3	Fore end ...	0	3
Butt ...	2	8	Butt ...	2	10
	5	8		5	12

Twenty Bores.

	lb.	oz.		lb.	oz.
22-inch barrels...	2	6	24-inch barrels...	2	8
Fore end ...	0	3	Fore end ...	0	3
Butt ...	2	3	Butt ...	2	5
	4	12		5	0

	lb.	oz.		lb.	oz.
26-inch barrels...	2	10	28-inch barrels...	2	12
Fore end ...	0	3	Fore end ...	0	3
Butt ...	2	7	Butt ...	2	9
	5	4		5	8

The above three weights are much under what are usually turned out, but they can be made to be perfectly safe and to shoot well. The light butts are obtained by boring them out to the required weights and using light furniture. The whole of the guns will balance well (that is behind the hinge joint) and handle pleasantly, and are given to shew how light guns can be built when required.

One who has Fired some 20,000 Shots at Marks.

Hammerless Guns and the Silver's Safety

Of all the stories that intertwine to make up the overall history of the sporting gun, how the vital imperative for safety was achieved is one of the strangest. Today we make use of the safety feature conferred on the drop down sporting gun by the fortuitous fact that, broken open, as if to load or remove spent cartridges, the gun is absolutely safe. So obvious and in such universal use is this method, that it is easy to forget that the adoption of this mode is of comparatively recent date.

As far as I am aware, no 19th century writer explained this situation, but we must remember that the vast majority of users of early breech loaders were converts from muzzle loading. With the old gun, removing an unfired charge from a fired gun was a dirty and time-consuming process, while even tight-fitting unfired caps can be difficult to remove. So perhaps that's where the fashion came from?

Looking at photographs of shooting parties of the Edwardian and even inter-war years, we see most guns were carried closed. From the accounts of numerous accidents, we realise they were also carried loaded.

The coming of the hammerless gun in the 70s and 80s served to exacerbate the situation, because, in most designs, the lockwork was put at full cock as the gun was opened, in which case the closed gun was also cocked.

In this respect, Arthur Lane seems to be just as guilty as his contemporaries. He admits as much in a letter published in *The Field* of August 13th 1881, part of which reads:

… Several times last season I caught myself in the act of getting over a hedge with the gun unbolted and once actually did so.

The popular contemporary solution to this problem was to apply some sort of lock-bolting mechanism so, in parallel with the hammerless gun, we see a rash of safety catches (see Chapter 6 of *The British Shotgun, Volume 2*.)

Arthur Lane's solution to this dilemma was typically pragmatic and he tells the story in part of a letter published in *The Field*.

ON LOADS AND LOADING

I am a man who likes to go with the times and try all new things in guns, and in point of fact, most of them reach me in some way or another. Wanting a new gun last year I went in for a hammerless one – Anson and Deeley's and I can't say I'm sorry that I did so, as it enabled me to give the system a thorough trial, and I shot with it the whole of last season; but I believe it would take a great deal to induce me to use it for another. I need hardly say after this that the gun now building for me by Mr W.W. Greener has rebounding locks with low hammers – than which I believe nothing yet has ever been brought our so thoroughly safe, handy, and convenient in every way. With this the most cursory glance discloses the condition the gun is in; with the other it is a matter of much more minute inspection, and you have no fumbling about on a cold day after wretched little bolts, knobs or buttons, and whether automatic or not that infernal bolt even with the most careful, is to a moral the wrong way at some time or other …

… I have not yet seen the gun mentioned by FRM (Messrs Silver's) but it appears from his description to comprise elements that may make it the best yet brought out.

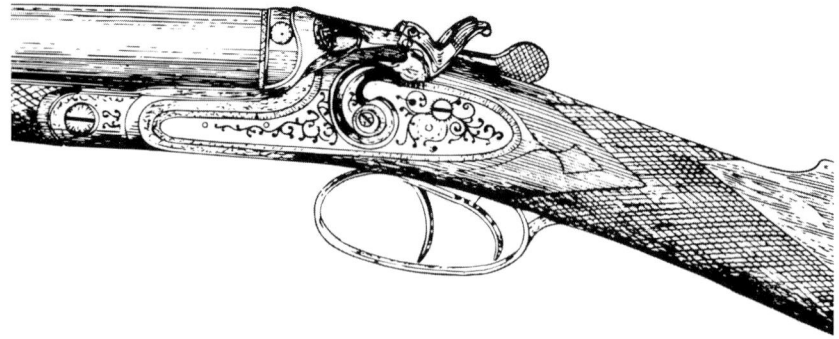

Greener's "First Quality" Hammer gun.

The last remark about the Silver's safety was prophetic, because, within a couple of years, Lane was to become a prolific advocate of the system. For instance, in *The Sporting Mirror* of June 1882, we find:

> This bolt is really what it purports to be, thoroughly and truly automatic, inasmuch as it works without any thought or act whatever on the part of the shooter. A look at the accompanying figure will at once shew how wonderfully simple is its construction. A single glance almost will explain it and its action. There is nothing to break, nothing to get out of order, and the only spring used it is impossible to put a breaking strain upon. The great beauty of this bolt is that the general and normal condition of the gun is one of *absolute* safety, without requiring anything to be done by the shooter to make it so. Barring a double fracture (a most remote chance) the gun cannot by any possibility be fired unless it is grasped by its "hand," so as to depress the lever. Should either of the scears (sic) by any accident be jarred out of the bents no accident can arise by pressure on the lever, as the gun cannot be fired until the opening lever has been so as to re-cock the hammers. And where one barrel only has been discharged the other is instantly

securely bolted on the shooter merely removing the grasp from the "hand" of the gun. And here, too, you are not bothered by any slides, studs, bolts or buttons whatever; the whole thing works entirely by itself. True, there is a hinged end to the lever which can be turned over the strap of the "trigger plate," or "break off," as the case may be, whereby the gun can be locked at safe at will. But the gun is so thoroughly safe as it stands that this seems to be really hardly required, though it is better this extra security should be there for use when needed.

THE FIELD, July 16th 1881

These events in the 1880s had an echo in the next decade when Arthur was put forward as being anti-hammerless gun. Writing in *The Field* of September 13th 1890, he countered this claim with the following:

HAMMERLESS GUNS

… But now all this has changed, great advances have been made in perfecting these guns, and almost endless improvements and alterations have been introduced in their construction and manufacture, and they are no longer liable to get out of order and break down on the smallest provocation; in fact they are at the present time quite different weapons, particularly in the way of safety, from what they were at the period at which I wrote upon them; and I am certain, had they been what they are now, those letters of caution of mine would never have appeared – there would have been no occasion for them …

THE FIELD, September 13th 1890

The trigger and tumbler bolting system that Messrs. Silver and Fletcher patented as No. 4210 of 1880, is but one of several involving Mr. Silver and is an example of a double bolting layout

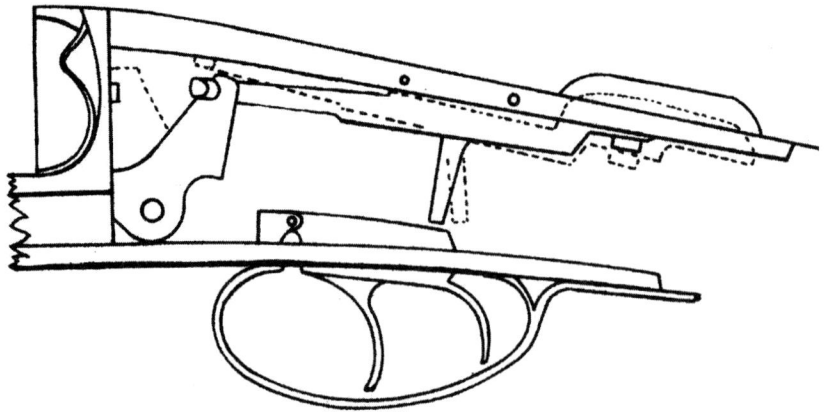

in which the movement of both the triggers and the tumblers is prevented by the apparatus and the gun so fitted can only be fired if it is grasped at the hand of the stock. This concept was old even in the 1880s, having first been used on muzzle loaders in the 1820s. It should be explained that the limb which blocks the trigger blades is a separate component and is hung on the front axle of the two in the top strap. It is fitted into a slot formed in the tumbler bolting limb and the pair of limbs are shaped so that, as the front of the tumbler bolt rises, the trigger bolt is lifted and so swung to the rear.

GUN ACCIDENTS PREVENTED
BY THE USE OF
S. W. SILVER & Co.'s
PATENT SAFETY
HAMMERLESS GUN.

All particulars on application to the Patentees and Manufacturers,

S. W. SILVER & CO.,
67, CORNHILL, LONDON.

The Last Letter

Having reproduced the first letter that Arthur Lane wrote to *The Field*, it is perhaps fitting that something should be included regarding his last – especially because, again, it gives us insight into his views.

So, in the issue of December 3rd 1898, we find another long epistle, the key paragraph of which reads:

> VELOCITY IN SHOT GUNS.
>
> SIR, - Among the old experimenters of the past generation, of whom I venture to consider myself one, we were always very careful to put forward nothing that we had not arrived at by actual experiment at the target – that is, we never ventured to put forward anything founded on analogy, deduction, or arithmetical or mathematical calculations. Now, it appears to me that there is at present a tendency to do this, particularly in the matter of velocities. We are now constantly told what this is with different charges at 20 yards, but we hear nothing of it at the actual target. Now, I submit that any calculations based on the velocity at that distance must be in most cases fallacious and misleading, as I propose to show.

This valid warning regarding 'armchair ballistics' in regard to the performance of any gun and cartridge combination at long range was totally ignored in the editorial response. Like a good politician, the editor wrote a somewhat supercilious piece on the great value of 20 yard velocities in the standardisation of the performance of shotgun propellant powders! Important though this is, it is not what Lane wrote about.

Sadly this was completely in keeping with *The Field* of the time which, regrettably gave a persistent impression of pompous self-importance.

Whoever wrote the response to Arthur's letter must have been aware of the lore surrounding the performance of shotgun barrels. In truth, this is an unstable mixture of fact with fancies which derive from a good day with a particular brand of cartridge, for instance.

The intervening century has only served to add to these. As so often was the case, the late Gough Thomas summed up the situation beautifully. He discovered, goodness knows where, that in the lore of the Native American, the shotgun was regarded as the female of the gun species, the rifle being the male. He offered this fact as the complete explanation of the unpredictability of the shotgun.

PART THREE

12-BORE 2¼-INCH FULL CHOKE AT 20 YARDS
Load : 33 grains Smokeless Diamond and 1 1/16 ounce of No. 6

Appendices

Appendix I

Milestones in the Life of A.J. Lane

The way in which this study has developed and the material discovered together conspired to make difficult the inclusion of details of Arthur Lane's life story.

To remedy this omission, and to present such information as has been assembled, the following list has been compiled.

- 1816 – Born 14th March. Parents: Thomas and Louisa (née Farindon). Youngest of three: Louisa, born 1805 and Farindon, born 1808.
- 1822 – Family moves to 'Farindons', Dormansland.
- 1832 – Mother dies.
- 1837 – Family leaves 'Farindons'.
- 1841 – Census. Arthur living with Aunt (?) at Great Coram Street, St. George's, Bloomsbury.
- 1843 – Date of *Fishing Manuscript*.
- 1845 – Marriage to Caroline Jones Ramsden.
- 1851 – Census. Visitor at 'Gibraltar Cottage', Speldhurst, Kent.
- 1854 – Son born: Arthur Evan Lane.
  Obtains patent No. 1536 for Breech Loading Rifle – address: 'The Ferns', King Charles Street, Surbiton.
- 1859 – Father dies, aged 89, at Brighton. No will.
- 1860 – First letter to *The Field*.
- 1861 – Census. Visitor at Inn, in Dulveston, Cornwall.
- 1871 – Census. Address: 34, Devonshire Place, Brighton – wife, cook and housemaid.

1876 –   Rear-Commodore of the Thames Sailing Club – boat: *Enchantress*.
1878 –   Loses sight in right eye.
Vice-Commodore of sailing club.
1881 –   Census. Address: 13, Buckingham Close, Brighton – wife, Annie Wilkins (cook), and Sarah Harrison (housemaid/domestic).
1884 –   Letters to *The Field* stop on 2nd August.
1888 –   Letters to *The Field* recommence on 21st April.
1891 –   Census. Address: 'Bentley', 14, Montpellier Villas, Brighton – wife and two servants.
1894 –   Wife dies in March.
1895 –   Marriage to Clara Carlotta in March.
1898 –   Last letter to *The Field*.
1901 –   Census. Address: 58, St. James Street, Brighton – wife, lady's companion, nurse, housemaid and cook.
1906 –   Death of Arthur James Lane, during the 2nd quarter of 1906 at 27, Lewis Close, Brighton.

Appendix II

Obituaries

To date the following have been located:

THE LATE MR. A.J. LANE

At one time no signature was more familiar to the shooting readers of *The Field* than that of "20,000 Shots". Mr. A.J. Norton Lane who adopted that signature, or to be more correct, "One who has Fired 20,000 Shots at Marks" took a very lively interest in the numerous experiments carried out by *The Field* and he contributed the results of many of his own trials with guns and gun powders. How greatly he associated himself with sports and pastimes of various kinds was plainly set down in the series of articles which he wrote to this paper during the year 1898 under the title of "Sporting Reminiscences and Anecdotes."

Failing sight and enfeebled health did not prevent him interesting himself in the modern methods adopted by shooters and experimenters and it is but a very few months since that his last letter appeared in our columns. With regret we learn that our old friend passed away at his residence at Brighton on Tuesday night from heart failure. He had reached the ripe age of ninety.

THE FIELD, May 12TH 1906 (Page 745)

The death is announced from Brighton of Mr. Arthur Norton-Lane, better known as "20,000 Shots," who must rank for all time as one of the most ingenious and thoughtful of the amateur enthusiasts who have studied the problems of the shot gun. Mr. Lane was in his 91st year, yet letters from his pen have appeared in the sporting press during the last year.

ARMS & EXPLOSIVES, June 1906 (Page 76)

Appendix III

A.J. Lane's Letters to *The Field*

VOL	PAGE	DATE	TITLE OR SUBJECT	SIZE
15	251	31/3/1860	Length of Gun Barrels	1040
22	129	1/8/1863	Trial of French Breech Loaders	200
45	42	16/1/1875	Re Choke Bore	200
45	109	30/1/1875	Re Choke Bore	500
45	125	6/2/1875	The Late Gun Trial	400
46	714	25/12/1875	Choke Bores, their Merits & Demerits	1,000
52	687	30/11/1878	Sticking Cartridge Cases	320
53	56	18/1/1879	Gun Chambering & Cheap Guns	780
53	111	1/2/1879	Small Bore Guns	455
53	163	15/2/1879	Proof Marks	455
53	243	1/3/1879	Boring Breech Loaders	650
53	282	15/3/1879	Boring Breech Loaders	260
53	475	26/4/1879	Game Licences	975
53	616	24/5/1879	Late Gun Trials	260
54	3	5/7/1879	Velocity & Large Shot	780
54	42	12/7/1879	Velocity of Shot	1.040
54	78	19/7/1879	Velocity of Shot	130
54	477	11/10/1879	Shooting with One Arm	228
54	544	25/10/1879	Short Barrels	385
55	270	6/3/1880	Concentrators & Schultze Powder	520
55	339	20/3/1880	Schultze Powders & Concentrators	553
55	439	10/4/1880	Honey Combing & Purified Oil	390
55	512	25/4/1880	Honey Combing in Barrels	260

56	13	3/7/1880	The Late Case of Balling with Schultze Powder	910
56	53	10/7/1880	Collectors Guns	585
56	94	17/7/1880	Schultze Powder etc.	585
56	290	21/8/1880	Collectors Guns	65
56	783	27/11/1880	English & Belgian Barrels	455
56	817	4/12/1880	English & Foreign Barrels	130
56	855	11/12/1880	Choice of a Gun	1,680
56	901	18/12/1880	Firing Wire Cartridges from Choke-Bored Guns	585
57	26	1/1/1881	Wear & Tear of Mr Greener's Guns	780
57	56	8/1/1881	Stocking & Choice of Guns etc	780
57	100	22/1/1881	Wear & Tear of Mr Greener's Guns	975
57	128	29/1/1881	Steel Barrels for Guns	650
57	176	5/2/1881	Wear & Tear of Guns	650
57	224	19/2/1881	Steel Barrels for Guns	390
57	224	19/2/1881	Stocking Guns etc	530
57	499	9/4/1881	Heel Plates etc	320
57	756	4/6/1881	Short Barrelled Guns	900
58	78/9	16/7/1881	On Loads & Loading	
58	192	6/8/1881	Choke Bores & Loading	530
58	229	13/8/1881	Hammerless Guns	900
58	355	3/9/1881	Cartridge Loading	200
58	355	3/9/1881	Hammerless Guns & Gun Accidents	130
58	401	10/9/1991	Long 20 Bores	1,300
58	479	1/10/1881	Long Guns v Short Guns	390
58	621	29/10/1881	Carrying Cartridges	530
58	687	12/11/1881	Long Shots	2,730
58	761	26/11/1881	Loading Wood Gun Powder	780
58	938	24/12/1881	Hawk Preservation & Rat Destruction	780
59	58	14/1/1882	Schultze Powder & Caps	720
59	186	11/2/1882	Schultze Powder & the Late Gun Accident	900

59	265	25/2/1882	The Silver Safety Bolt	450
59	285	4/3/1882	Kynoch's New Perfect Cartridge Case	1,300
59	325	11/3/1882	Choked & Cylinder Barrels Schultze Powder	650
59	325	11/3/1882	Wood Powder	150
59	676	20/5/1882	Wild Shots	260
60	83	15/7/1882	Kynoch's "Perfects"	780
60	124	22/7/1882	Kynoch's "Perfects"	910
60	215	12/8/1882	Kynoch's "Perfects"	650
60	409	16/9/1882	Kynoch's "Perfects" in Converted Guns	
60	446	23/9/1882	Kynoch's "Perfects" in Converted Guns	2,210
60	471	30/9/1882	Ford's Boring for Kynoch's "Perfects"	1,170
61	680	26/5/1883	Morris Tubes	1,170
61	827	23/6/1883	Sham Damascus	650
62	288	25/8/1883	Trial of E.C. Powder at Kynoch's	2,470
62	380	15/9/1883	Kynoch's "Perfects"	1,040
62	441	29/9/1883	Charges for Guns	520
62	657	10/11/1883	Missfires in Greener Guns	650
62	673	17/11/1883	Letter in reply to Editor's Criticism	130
62	773	8/12/1883	Modern Explosives	1,300
62	841	15/12/1883	On the Proof of Guns	2,730
63	65	19/1/1884	Silvers' Automatic Bolt	520
63	343	8/3/1884	Trial of Explosives	1,170
63	378	15/3/1884	Ground Game Act	2,000
63	452	29/3/1884	Steel Traps	1,560
64	4	5/7/1884	Steel Barrels	910
64	155	2/8/1884	Steel Barrels	520
71	581	21/4/1888	Small Bore Guns	1,040
71	634	5/5/1888	Small Bore Guns	1,300
71	663	12/5/1888	Small Bore Guns	1,040
71	700	19/5/1888	Small Bore Guns	1,040
71	855	16/6/1888	Gun Barrels	910

71	930	30/6/1888	Damascus or Steel	1,170
72	3	7/7/1888	Steel v Damascus	
72	76/7	14/7/1888	Steel v Damascus	910
72	82	21/7/1888	Steel v Damascus	1,040
72	123/4	28/7/1888	Steel v Damascus	1,170
72	307/8	25/8/1888	Steel v Damascus	1,950
72	352	8/9/1888	Steel v Damascus	1,000
72	495	6/10/1888	Shooting Game at Long Range	1,040
72	522	13/10/1888	Shooting Game at Long Range	1,820
72	583	20/10/1888	Gun Fit	1,040
72	629	3/11/1888	Cylinders v Choke	1,170
72	629	3/11/1888	Long Shots	130
72	629	3/11/1888	Gun Fit	130
72	732	17/11/1888	Cylinders v Choke	1,040
72	732	17/11/1888	Spreader Loads	1,040
72	739	24/11/1888	Spreader Loads	520
73	12/13	5/1/1889	Airwaves around Projectiles	715
73	69	19/1/1889	Boat Shaped Bullets	260
73	70	19/1/1889	Hammerless Guns	260
73	197	9/2/1889	Perfect Cartridges	715
73	197	9/2/1889	Breech Actions	260
73	212	16/2/1889	Repeating Shotguns	1,150
73	386	16/3/1889	Doll Head Action (sic)	390
73	429	30/3/1889	Smoke	975
73	465	6/4/1889	Close Time for Hares	585
73	465	6/4/1889	Guns of our Ancestors	520
73	577	22/4/1889	Shooting Ball out of Smooth Bores	1,040
74	204	10/8/1889	Length of Gun Barrel & its Influence on Shooting	910
74	261	17/8/1889	Length of Gun Barrels	715
74	347	7/9/1889	Short Barrels	1,100

74	449	28/9/1889	Short Barrels	2,200
74	534	12/10/1889	Short Barrels	1,100
74	580	26/10/1889	Shooting birds Overhead	1,430
74	674	9/11/1889	Shooting birds Overhead	715
74	867	21/11/1889	Kynoch's Perfect Cases	585
75	66	11/1/1890	The Patterns of Sporting Guns	715
75	209	8/2/1890	Burst Rifle	780
75	225	15/2/1890	28 Bores	1,820
75	303	1/3/1890	28 Bores	1,170
75	331	8/3/1890	Patterns of Guns for Everyday Work	1,628
75	367	15/3/1890	Loads for Small Bore Guns	1,300
75	412	22/3/1890	Guns for Everyday Work	2,080
75	448	28/3/1890	Guns for Everyday Work	130
75	478	5/4/1890	Guns for Everyday Work	1,040
75	736	17/5/1889	Guns for Everyday Work & their Loading	2,600
75	821	7/6/1890	Planting Coverts near the Sea	1,690
75	944	28/6/1890	Long Range Shooting with Guns	975
76	403	13/9/1890	Hammerless Guns	585
76	631	25/10/1890	Fouling of 28 Bore Guns	845
77	4	3/1/1891	Leading of Shotguns & Short Barrels	1,040
77	287	28/2/1891	Recapping Perfects, Anvil Loading etc	910
77	390	14/3/1891	Utility of Try Guns	2,730
77	439	28/3/1891	Fit of Gun	130
78	510	3/10/1891	Pistol Shooting Extraordinary	910
78	594	17/10/1891	Fords Patent Wads	585
78	654	31/10/1891	Loading Cartridges with Nitro Powder	650
79	165	6/2/1892	Glancing of Shot - Soft and Hard	910
79	293	27/2/1892	Strength of Gun Actions	715
79	386/7	12/3/1892	Strength of Gun Actions	1,690
79	463	26/3/1892	Long & Short Cartridges & Chambers	455
80	241	6/8/1892	Soft Felt Wads	715

80	303	20/8/1892	Remarkably early appearance of Grouse	390
80	332	27/8/1892	Remarkably early appearance of Grouse	130
80	833	26/11/1892	Modification of load for Choke Bores & Long Range Shots	2,400
80	872	3/12/1892	Guns Damaged by Nitro Powders	715
80	951/2	17/12/1892	Guns Broken by Nitro Powders	1,625
80	993	31/12/1892	Accidents to Guns	1,690
81	73	21/1/1893	Broken Breech Actions & Gun Barrels	1,560
83	399	24/3/1894	Loads & Patterns for Moderate Shots	1,170
86	226	10/8/1895	The Crushing of Shot within the Gun Barrel	780
86	402	7/9/1895	Compression of Shot in Gun Barrels	450
86	595	12/10/1895	Small Charges of Shot	520
88	4	4/7/1896	The Late Gun Trials	1,430
89	365	13/3/1897	Length of Barrels	1,000
89	415	20/3/1897	Length of Barrels	350
89	453	27/3/1897	Length of Barrels	260
90	183	31/7/1897	Fords Patent Cartridges	200
90	665	23/10/1897	Curious old Rifle	96
90	835	27/11/1897	Guns for Wild Game etc	1,300
90	939	11/12/1897	Guns & Loads	260
91	24	1/1/1898	Light Guns	680
91	91	15/1/1898	Steel Barrels	1.560
91	142	29/1/1898	How to Carry a Gun	390
91	657	30/4/1898	Gun Headache	585
92	725	29/10/1898	Cast off in Shotguns	320
92	921	3/12/1898	Shooting Accidents	200

Appendix IV

Notes from A.J. Lane's Letters to *The Field*

It was obligatory in this study to read all of Arthur Lane's voluminous correspondence. The reward for this effort was a haul of titbits of autobiography and other snippets.

Where possible these have been included in the main text, but there remains a residue that is well worth recording. Given that they form such a random group, they can only be recorded in order of publication.

Volume 57, Page 26

DOC CARVER'S GUN
Sent for examination. Reputed to have fired 80,000 shots and never cleaned or repaired. Very slightly off the face with glass dust in the action.

Volume 57, Page 56

BURST GUN
At Cambridge I once fell in with a man on a pike fishing trip with a hook to his left arm. On asking him how he lost his hand he told me he had been a fen man and on one occasion in shooting at a flash of fen birds he rested his heavy gun on his son's head, a lad of ten or twelve years old – and held his left hand at the guard. On firing the gun had burst and his hand was utterly shattered but the boy was unhurt.

Volume 58, Page 621

SHOOTING WAISTCOAT: CARRYING CARTRIDGES

For years have had my shooting waistcoats made with four good deep pockets with largish flaps, each pocket long enough to take seven No. 12 cartridges or eight No. 16, placed vertically.

Volume 60, Page 471

HARDING GUN

Gun belonging to his father by Harding - ... the thread (of the breech) became so worn and scored that at last on washing it out with a tight rod, three or five jets of water were projected past the plug.

Volume 74, Page 534

SQUIRES SHORT BARRELS

The elder Squires of Whitechapel (who had been apprenticed to the celebrated Fullard) thoroughly understood short barrels, and was another ally of mine.

Volume 74, Page 674

THROWN TURNIPS

Letter in praise of thrown turnips for practice, no glass fragments and targets always available at every country house.

Volume 75, Page 412 (Part of a letter)

GUNS FOR EVERYDAY WORK

There is a man who has been a profession shot, but is now the shooter and tryer at G. Kynoch and Co.'s Ammunition Factory. His name is Cornelius Dixon. Taking him all round, for rifle, pistol and shotgun, he is probably the best shot out. With a single ball he can stop running rabbits or flying birds with the most wonderful certainty. With an oval bore rifle of mine, presented to me by Mr. C. Lancaster, I have seen him break about nine out of ten glass balls thrown up, away from or across him.

Volume 86 (Part of a letter about Small Charges of Shot)

For my last two or three seasons I carried a 32 bore, just turning the scale at 3lb built especially for my old age by Mr. William Ford, and it was my own fault if I did not kill forty seven or forty eight out of every fifty shots up to 40 yards with 3/4 oz of No. 5. In fact it did the work for me quite as well, if not better, than any 12 of 6lb or 7lb, the great thing being that I never got tired with it and so began to bag or miss my game altogether.

Volume 88, Page 4 (Part of a letter)

THE LATE GUN TRIALS

By way of speaking of kicking, I may mention that some sixty five years ago when a lad of fifteen or sixteen, I possessed a gun by the famous old Baker of Whitechapel. It had previously belonged to my uncle, Major H.B. Lane, RA., the well known Commander of the Congreve Rocket Brigade in the Peninsular War. This gun had the Baker patent breech which consisted a perfectly round chamber capable of holding nearly a dram of powder, into which the touch hole communicated; the first chamber was connected by a passage about 1/8inch in diameter with an outer chamber, very like Joe Manton's. Talk about kicking like a horse, this gun may be said to have kicked like an elephant. I was a pretty wiry strong lad, but it punished me awfully in the way of bruised cheek and shoulder. I think the load I used was 2drs and 1¼ oz and so loaded it was all I could do to hold it. My good old father saw me shoot with it one day and finding me pretty nearly turned round at every discharge took it away from me … It subsequently went into the hands of a gamekeeper, but he was compelled to give it up as he said it shook him all to pieces.

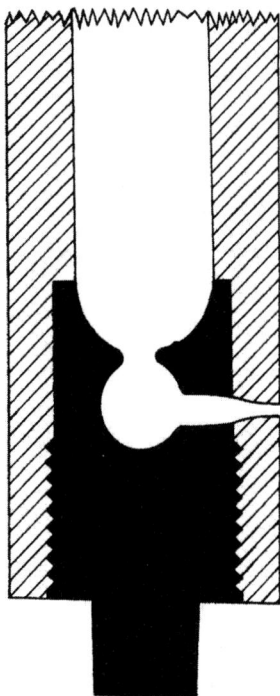

The Baker breech from the firm's trade label.

The description of its use suggests high or even dangerous pressure.

Appendix V

Other Writings by A. J. Lane

The Sporting Mirror, **May 1882.**

"A BAULK MATCH AT PIGEONS"

Set in rural Essex in the 1840s, this is said to be the true story of a live pigeon trap match. Arthur Lane tells how, by gamesmanship, he was able to outwit a practised "Sharp".

The Sporting Mirror, **September 1882.**

"AN ELOPEMENT WHICH DID NOT COME OFF"

Arthur Lane wrote this fanciful, fictional piece which is long-winded and rambling. It is, however, crammed to excess with details culled from his first-hand knowledge of the boating and shooting worlds.

THE SHOOTING NOTES

At several points in some of the other writings of A.J.L., there is mention of records that he had kept of his various experiments. Most regrettably, this no longer seems to exist. Doubtless it was destroyed because, to a casual observer, a collection of notebooks or even ledgers would be little more than lists of numbers. To us, the brief notes that must have accompanied these numbers would have been a gold mine of information.

THE FISHING MANUSCRIPT

In 1995 this manuscript was published by The Medlar Press as *The Diary of A.J. Lane*, in two volumes; a facsimile and a typed transcript. Despite a fabricated title-page, this was not a diary, but a hand-written manuscript describing freshwater fish and fishing methods, possibly intended for future publication. The publishers knew nothing about the identity or background of the author. That Lane, the shooting man, and Lane, the angling "diarist," were the same person only came to light when I first approached my publisher, Paul Morgan, who recognised the name and made the connection.

Unfortunately, the author of the commentary accompanying the Medlar Press edition is far too keen to parade his own knowledge, wide-ranging and erudite as it undoubtedly must be. Thus we are regaled with all the facts in the Lane text which modern research has proved to be wrong, and even more irritatingly, it was thought necessary to quibble with every spelling variation and minor point of Lane's nineteenth century grammar.

Lane's colour plates of fish and flies are well executed. As a young man he had hoped to become a professional artist, but was obliged to follow the same career as his father, becoming a solicitor.

Lane was widowed in 1894 and in 1895 at the age of 79 he married again. He new wife was named Clara. His original fishing manuscript carries an inscription or dedication, "With my sincere affection, Clara Norton Lane." He was known (at least, in later life) as Arthur Norton-Lane and he appears as such in the 1901 census, when he was living in Brighton. He was referred to as Mr. Norton Lane by Lord Rossmore in his biography, *Things I Can Tell* (1912).